State Management with React Hooks

Cristian Salcescu

State Management
with React Hooks

State Management with React Hooks

Cristian Salcescu

Copyright © 2023 Cristian Salcescu

ISBN-13: 979-8378917396

History:

February 2023 First Edition, Paperback

Contents

Chapter 18: Takeaways

Introduction

React innovates UI rendering by enabling the creation of components as functions and forcing immutable values. We can simply build functions that take data and transform it into UI elements. We call these stateless functional components.

React is a library for creating the user interface. The visual representation depends on state data. Any changes to the state data are shown on the screen. This is why React is said to be also a state management UI library.

Not only components are functions but we can also create such function components storing state. These function components re-render themselves once the internal state changes.

This kind of function components storing state is the focus of this book. They are called stateful components.

Chapter 01: Understanding State

What is state? Is state just data?

These are questions we are going to explore in this first chapter. We will implement a simple toggle button component and then draw some conclusions about state.

Is This State?

Let's start by creating a function component displaying a button with the text On or Off depending on the isOn variable.

```
function ToggleButton() {
  const isOn = true;
  return <button>{isOn ? "On" : "Off"}</button>;
}

export default ToggleButton;
```

The function component declares a constant isOn holding the current status of the button and then uses conditional rendering to display a button with the right text, On or Off.

What do you say, can we think of the isOn variable as storing state data at this point?

No. The isOn does not change. It does not represent state data.

Next, we give the ability to the isOn variable to be changed by creating it with the let declaration.

```
function ToggleButton() {
  let isOn = true;

  function toggle() {
    isOn = !isOn;
    console.log(isOn);
  }

  return (
    <button onClick={toggle}>
      {isOn ? "On" : "Off"}
    </button>
  );
}
```

```
export default ToggleButton;
```

The `toggle` function handles the `onClick` event of the toggle button. When the button is clicked the boolean value stored in the `isOn` variable changes and then the new value is logged to the console.

You may notice that even though the variable changes, the HTML is not updated.

What do you think? Does the `isOn` variable store state at this point?

Not yet. Even if state represents data that can change, modifying that data should be reflected on the screen. The value stored in the `isOn` variable changes but the screen does not show this modification.

State Hook

React allows us to define such variables storing state and updating the screen when they change using the `useState` hook utility.

The `useState` hook function takes the initial value and returns an array with two elements. The first value gives read access to the state value, and the second element is a setter function and allows changing that state. This setter function modifies the state value and invokes the component function. By doing so it changes the HTML.

In the next example, the `isOn` variable allows us to read the state and the `setIsOn` function changes that state and re-renders the HTML by

invoking the `ToogleButton` function. The state variable is initialized with
`false`.

```
import { useState } from "react";

function ToggleButton() {
  const [isOn, setIsOn] = useState(false);

  console.log(isOn);

  function toggle() {
    setIsOn(!isOn);
  }

  return (
    <button onClick={toggle}>
      {isOn ? "On" : "Off"}
    </button>
  );
}
```

```
export default ToggleButton;
```

By adding a `console.log` inside the `ToggleButton` component function
we can notice that the function is called every time the toggle button is
clicked.

There are two ways to invoke the `setIsOn` function. It can be called with
the new value and this is what was done in the `toggle` handler.

The `setIsOn` can also be invoked with an updater function taking the
current state and returning a new state value. The next `toggleValue`
function is an updater function.

Instead of passing the new value to the `setIsOn` function we can pass the
`toggleValue` function that computes the new state value.

```
import { useState } from "react";

function toggleValue(value) {
  return !value;
}
```

```
function ToggleButton() {
  const [isOn, setIsOn] = useState(false);

  function toggle() {
    setIsOn(toggleValue);
  }

  return (
    <button onClick={toggle}>
      {isOn ? "On" : "Off"}
    </button>
  );
}

export default ToggleButton;
```

State

This simple toggle component we built so far is helpful for understanding a few attributes of what is a state variable.

Here are the main attributes of state data:

- the data is stored
- it can be changed
- the change is reflected on the screen

At this point, we can say that state is data that is stored, that can be changed, and whose transformation is represented on the screen.

Key Notes

- Data that does not changes is not state.
- The state data changes and when that happens the function component re-renders and reflects the new value on the screen.
- The state data can be declared inside function components using the useState hook.
- The state can be changed by providing a new state value or an updater function. The updater function takes the current state and returns the new state.

Chapter 02: Immutable State Data

In addition to introducing components as functions, React implements another core functional programming technique, immutability, and as such has brought in the use of immutable values.

What is an immutable value?

An immutable value is one that once created cannot be changed.

Ok, but then what does immutable state actually mean? Does it mean that state cannot be changed?

We just said that state is data that can be changed. Immutability implies that the value stored in the state variable should be treated as immutable.

Let's give some examples to make things clear.

Changing Primitives

First, primitives like strings, numbers, and booleans are immutable so when storing such values we don't have to do anything special when changing the value.

As we noticed in the toggle button example, modifying the boolean value is straightforward.

```
const [isOn, setIsOn] = useState(false);

function toggle() {
  setIsOn(!isOn);
}
```

Changing Objects

Now consider storing an object that has the `isOn` property. Changing the `isOn` property of the original object is wrong and React cannot detect the modification in the state variable.

The new state value is not shown on the screen in the following incorrect example.

```
import { useState } from "react";

function ToggleButton() {
  const [state, setState] = useState({
    isOn: false
  });

  function toggle() {
    state.isOn = !state.isOn;
    console.log(state);
    setState(state);
  }

  return (
    <button onClick={toggle}>
      {state.isOn ? "On" : "Off"}
    </button>
  );
}
```

```
export default ToggleButton;
```

Objects in JavaScript are mutable. Treating an object as being immutable implies creating a changed copy when doing a modification.

One simple way to make a copy of a plain object is to use the spread operator (. . .). Here is an example.

```
const newState = { ...state };
```

The following code makes a copy of the existing state object and then changes the `isOn` property.

```
const newState = { ...state };
newState.isOn = !state.isOn;
```

We can clone the initial state object and change the property with a single line of code.

```
const newState = { ...state, isOn: !state.isOn };
```

Below is an example of how we can correctly write the `toggle` handler using a changed copy of the state object.

```
function toggle() {
  const newState = { ...state, isOn: !state.isOn };
  setState(newState);
}
```

Updater Function

Nonetheless, a better option is to pass an updater function to the `setState` function. The updater function gives access to the current state variable. In a later chapter, we will see why this is the better option. The `prevState` input in the updater function always reflects the last value of the state object while direct access to the state variable is troublesome in some specific cases.

```
function toggle() {
  setState((prevState) =>
    ({ ...prevState, isOn: !prevState.isOn }));
}
```

Below is the full logic for the `ToggleButton` component implemented using a plain object with one boolean property as state data.

```
import { useState } from "react";

function toggle() {
  setState((prevState) =>
    ({ ...prevState, isOn: !prevState.isOn }));
}

function ToggleButton() {
  const [state, setState] = useState({
    isOn: false
  });

  function toggle() {
    setState(toogleIsOn);
```

```
  }

  return (
    <button onClick={toggle}>
      {state.isOn ? "On" : "Off"}
    </button>
  );
}

export default ToggleButton;
```

Key Notes

- Storing and changing primitives, like numbers, strings, and booleans is straightforward as they are immutable.
- Modifying objects implies creating a changed copy of them.
- The spread operator can be used for cloning objects.

Chapter 03: Form

In the next chapter, we start discussing how to handle the state for the input fields in a form.

But first what is the purpose of an HTML form?

An HTML form is used to collect the user input. Usually, this user input is then sent to the server for processing. The form element includes different types of input elements, such as text fields, text areas, dropdowns, checkboxes, radio buttons, submit buttons, etc.

This chapter covers textbox and password management. In the next chapters, we will look at other form inputs.

Before we get started, why do we need state for the input fields anyway? Can't we just directly access an input field and get or change its value?

This is not a good approach. In React as in many other UI frameworks, the practice is to modify the state in order to change the UI. Also in order to read data from the UI, we just read the associated state data. That implies that the associated state data is in sync with the input value. For that, we need to change the state value whenever the input value changes.

An input that has an associated state variable is called a controlled input. A controlled input has both the `value/checked` and the `onChange` properties defined. We will see later what this looks like.

There are two ways we can do this. We can either have an associated state variable for each input or we can create a single state object with a property for each input.

Form Component

Let's consider a simple form asking you to fill in your username and password.

```
function LoginForm() {
  return (
    <form>
      <div>
        <label>Username:</label>
        <input type="text" />
      </div>
      <div>
        <label>Password:</label>
        <input type="password" />
      </div>
      <div>
        <button type="submit">Login</button>
      </div>
    </form>
  );
}
```

```
export default LoginForm;
```

Besides the text and the password inputs, we need also a button to send the form to the server. Notice that the button element has the type submit. The default behavior of such a button is to submit all the form data to the server and refresh the page.

There are two ways to avoid this refresh default behavior. We can just change the type of the element to be button.

```
<button type="button">Login</button>
```

The other option is to use the preventDefault method on the event object when handling the onClick/onSubmit events. Below is such a handler function.

```
const submit = () => {
  e.preventDefault();
}
```

The submit function is the event handler for the login button.

```
<button onClick={submit}>Login</button>
```

Associated State Variables

Next, we take the first approach and create an associated state variable for each input field. There are two inputs in the form so here are the two variables storing the state for them.

```
const [username, setUsername] = useState('');
const [password, setPassword] = useState('');
```

And here is how we can associate a state variable with the related input. Below is the username text input reading its data from the state variable and updating the same state variable when the input changes.

```
<input
 type="text"
 value={username}
 onChange={(e) => setUsername(e.target.value)}
/>
```

The value in a text input is defined using the `value` attribute.

When the text input changes, the `onChange` event is triggered and the new value can be accessed on the event object by reading the `e.target.value` property.

In a similar way, we can associate the password input with the corresponding state variable.

```
<input
 type="password"
 value={password}
 onChange={(e) => setPassword(e.target.value)}
/>
```

Submitting

Now, when the form is submitted the state variables have the current values of the input fields.

```
import { useState } from "react";

function LoginForm() {
  const [username, setUsername] = useState("");
```

```
const [password, setPassword] = useState("");

const submit = () => {
  console.log({ username, password });
};

//...
<button type="button" onClick={submit}>
//...
}
```

Adding a New Input

Next, let's follow the previous steps and add a new checkbox input.

We previously saw that the state variables for text inputs were storing strings. What kind of data type should we use for checkboxes?

Indeed, booleans.

First, we defined the associated state variable.

```
const [rememberMe, setRememberMe] = useState(false);
```

Then we associate the state variable with the checkbox input field.

```
<input
 type="checkbox"
 checked={rememberMe}
 onChange={(e) => setRememberMe(e.target.checked)}
/>
```

Notice that for the checkbox input instead of using the **value** property we need to use the **checked** property. Also when the checkbox changes the new status can be accessed on the event object by reading the **e.target.checked** property.

Here is the **LoginForm** component defined so far.

```
import { useState } from "react";

function LoginForm() {
  const [username, setUsername] = useState("");
  const [password, setPassword] = useState("");
  const [rememberMe, setRememberMe] = useState(false);
```

```jsx
const submit = () => {
  console.log({ username, password, rememberMe });
};

return (
  <form>
    <div>
      <label>Username:</label>
      <input
        type="text"
        value={username}
        onChange={(e) => setUsername(e.target.value)}
      />
    </div>
    <div>
      <label>Password:</label>
      <input
        type="password"
        value={password}
        onChange={(e) => setPassword(e.target.value)}
      />
    </div>
    <div>
      <input
        type="checkbox"
        checked={rememberMe}
        onChange={(e) => setRememberMe(e.target.checked)}
      />
      <label>Remember me:</label>
    </div>
    <div>
      <button type="button" onClick={submit}>
        Login
      </button>
    </div>
  </form>
);
}
```

```
export default LoginForm;
```

A Single State Object

Now, let's take the second approach and create a single state object. The state object contains a property for each field.

```
const [state, setState] = useState({
  username: "",
  password: "",
  rememberMe: false
});
```

We associate each state property with an input. Here is the case for the username input.

```
<input
  type="text"
  value={state.username}
  onChange={(e) => {}}
/>
```

Now there is a single `setState` function updating all of the state object properties. How are we going to update the state object this time?

One thing we can do is ask for the name of the property to change. Below is a possible `setField` handler that updates a single property from the state object. It gets the name of the property to modify and the new value.

```
const setField = (name, value) => {}
```

One important thing to remember is that state value should be treated as immutable.

Remember that the object literal syntax allows computed property names. It lets you put an expression between brackets []. That expression is computed and used as the property name.

Here is how we can create a new copy of the state object and change a property on it using a computed property.

```
const setField = (name, value) => {
  setState({ ...state, [name]: value });
};
```

As already discussed a better option is to pass an updater function to the setState function.

```
const setField = (name, value) => {
  setState((prevState) => ({ ...prevState, [name]: value }));
};
```

Below the setField function is used to update the property for the username input.

```
<input
  type="text"
  value={state.username}
  onChange={(e) => setField("username", e.target.value)}
/>
```

In a similar way, we can set the other inputs. Here is the password field.

```
<input
  type="password"
  value={state.password}
  onChange={(e) => setField("password", e.target.value)}
/>
```

Next is the remember me checkbox.

```
<input
  type="checkbox"
  checked={state.rememberMe}
  onChange={(e) => setField("rememberMe", e.target.checked)}
/>
```

In the submit handler, the state object gives access to all the form inputs' values.

```
const submit = () => {
  console.log(state);
};
```

Using the Name Attribute

We can simplify the setField handler by having a name attribute on each input. Instead of taking both the name and the value as inputs, in the handler function, we can have a single parameter, the change event itself.

Then we extract the name and the value from that event object. Here is how it can be done.

```
const setField = (e) => {
  const name = e.target.name;
  const value = e.target.type === "checkbox" ?
    e.target.checked : e.target.value;

  setState((prevState) => ({ ...prevState, [name]: value }));
};
```

Notice that we need to use the `e.target.checked` property to access the new value when dealing with a checkbox. If the input triggering the event is a checkbox (`e.target.type === "checkbox"`) then we need to use the `e.target.checked` property otherwise we can rely on the `e.target.value` property.

Below is the username input having the **name** attribute and using the new `setField` handler.

```
<input
  type="text"
  name="username"
  value={state.username}
  onChange={setField}
/>
```

Below is the full code for the `LoginForm` component.

```
import { useState } from "react";

function LoginForm() {
  const [state, setState] = useState({
    username: "",
    password: "",
    rememberMe: false
  });

  const setField = (e) => {
    const name = e.target.name;
    const value = e.target.type === "checkbox" ?
      e.target.checked : e.target.value;
```

```
  setState((prevState) => ({ ...prevState, [name]: value }));
};

const submit = () => {
  console.log(state);
};

return (
  <form>
    <div>
      <label>Username:</label>
      <input
        type="text"
        name="username"
        value={state.username}
        onChange={setField}
      />
    </div>
    <div>
      <label>Password:</label>
      <input
        type="password"
        name="password"
        value={state.password}
        onChange={setField}
      />
    </div>
    <div>
      <input
        type="checkbox"
        name="rememberMe"
        checked={state.rememberMe}
        onChange={setField}
      />
      <label>Remember me:</label>
    </div>
    <div>
      <button type="button" onClick={submit}>
        Login
      </button>
```

```
    </div>
  </form>
);
}

export default LoginForm;
```

Key Notes

- Inputs having an associated state variable are called controlled inputs. They have both the `onChange` and `value/checked` properties defined.
- The state variable is always in sync with the associated input value.
- Textboxes, text areas, numbers, and password inputs are handled in a similar way.

Chapter 04: Form State Custom Hook

This chapter looks at how to reuse logic related to state management using what are called custom hooks.

First, what kind of state management logic can be reused?

For example, the `setField` function can be reused in several forms.

```
const setField = (e) => {
  const name = e.target.name;
  const value =
    e.target.type === "checkbox"
      ? e.target.checked
      : e.target.value;

  setState((prevState) => ({ ...prevState, [name]: value }));
};
```

Creating a Custom Hook

Let's create a custom hook encapsulating that logic.

What is a custom hook?

A custom hook is a function that starts with the prefix `"use"` and uses other standard hooks like `useState`.

Our hook will be named `useForm`.

Consider the state management logic from the `From` component.

```
function LoginForm() {
```

```
const [state, setState] = useState({
  username: "",
  password: "",
  rememberMe: false
});

const setField = (e) => {
  const name = e.target.name;
  const value = e.target.type === "checkbox" ?
    e.target.checked : e.target.value;
  setState((prevState) => ({ ...prevState, [name]: value }));
};

const submit = () => {
  console.log(state);
};

//...
}
```

We can encapsulate all this logic inside a new useForm hook and then reuse it. In order to keep it simple, the submit function will not be in the new custom hook.

Here is what the useForm hook may look like at this point.

```
function useForm() {
  const [state, setState] = useState({
    username: "",
    password: "",
    rememberMe: false
  });

  const setField = (e) => {
    const name = e.target.name;
    const value = e.target.type === "checkbox" ?
      e.target.checked : e.target.value;
    setState((prevState) => ({ ...prevState, [name]: value }));
  };
}
```

The custom hook is incomplete now. It should return something for the client code to use. What should it return?

We can return the **state** object and the **setField** handler function. The client code can read the state using the **state** variable and can change it using the **setField**. **setField** is used as an event handler for the change event.

```
function useForm() {
  const [state, setState] = useState({
    username: "",
    password: "",
    rememberMe: false
  });

  const setField = (e) => {}

  return [state, setField];
}
```

Another problem with our hook is that it is not generic. It always creates a state object with three hard-coded properties. Let's make it generic by taking the initial values of the fields as a plain input object.

```
import { useState } from "react";

function useForm(fields) {
  const [state, setState] = useState(fields);

  const setField = (e) => {};

  return [state, setField];
}

export default useForm;
```

That's it. Below is how it can be used.

```
import useForm from "./useForm";

function LoginForm() {
  const [state, setField] = useForm({
    username: "",
```

```
    password: "",
    rememberMe: false
  });

  const submit = () => {
    console.log(state);
  };

  return (
    <form></form>
  );
}

export default LoginForm;
```

Key Notes

- The state management logic can be reused in several components by encapsulating it inside a custom hook.
- A custom hook is a function having the "use" prefix and holding logic that makes use of other standard hooks.

Chapter 05: Drop-Down List

Next, we look at how to handle the state for another common input, the drop-down list.

First, we need a list of values to render inside the drop-down element. Consider a list of country names.

```
["Italy", "Spain", "Greece"]
```

Should this list of values be stored as state data?

Let's think about it. Do the drop-down options change? If they don't then it is not state data. In this case, it can be defined as a constant.

```
const options = ["Italy", "Spain", "Greece"];
```

Rendering the List

Now let's render the list of options on the screen. We do that using the `map` array method that transforms a list of strings into several `option` elements. Each string item is mapped to an `option` element.

For each `option` element, the `value` and the `text` attributes are defined. In our case, they are represented using the same value, but they can take different values.

```
const options = ["Italy", "Spain", "Greece"];

function DropdownForm() {
  return (
    <form>
      <select>
        {options.map((value) => (
          <option value={value} key={value}>
            {value}
          </option>
        ))}
      </select>
    </form>
  );
}

export default DropdownForm;
```

State

Is there something that does change?

Yes, it is. The selected value from the list does change. The selected value is state data. We declare it as state using the `useState` hook. Also, we can initialize it with the first value from the option list.

```
import { useState } from "react";

const [selected, setSelected] = useState(options[0]);
```

The `selected` variable allows us to read the state and the `setSelected` setter function enables us to modify that state and re-render the component.

To associate the `selected` state data with the drop-down input we make it a controlled input. A controlled input has both the `value` and `onChange` properties defined.

```
import { useState } from "react";

const options = ["Italy", "Spain", "Greece"];

function DropdownForm() {
  const [selected, setSelected] = useState(options[0]);

  return (
    <form>
      <select
       value={selected}
       onChange={e => setSelected(e.target.value)}>
        {options.map((value) => (
          <option value={value} key={value}>
            {value}
          </option>
        ))}
      </select>
    </form>
  );
}

export default DropdownForm;
```

The currently selected value in the drop-down can be extracted from the change event by accessing the `e.target.value` property.

Now when the form is submitted, the `selected` state variable gives access to the chosen value in the drop-down.

```
function DropdownForm() {
  const [selected, setSelected] = useState(options[0]);

  const submit = () => {
    console.log(selected);
  };

  return (
    <form>
      <!-- ... -->
      <button type="button" onClick={submit}>
        Submit
```

```
      </button>
    </form>
  );
}
```

```
export default DropdownForm;
```

That is all we need to do. As you notice, managing a drop-down list is similar to managing a textbox input. Below is the complete code.

```
import { useState } from "react";

const options = ["Italy", "Spain", "Greece"];

function DropdownForm() {
  const [selected, setSelected] = useState(options[0]);

  const submit = () => {
    console.log(selected);
  };

  return (
    <form>
      <select
       value={selected}
       onChange={(e) => setSelected(e.target.value)}>
         {options.map((value) => (
          <option value={value} key={value}>
            {value}
          </option>
         ))}
      </select>
      <button type="button" onClick={submit}>
        Submit
      </button>
    </form>
  );
}

export default DropdownForm;
```

Key Notes

- The selected value in a drop-down list represents state data.
- The options in a drop-down list are not state data if they do not change.

Chapter 06: Checkbox List vs List of Radio Buttons

Next, we look at how to manage a list of radio buttons vs a list of checkboxes.

In both cases, we need the list of options to display on the screen. Below is such a list.

```
[
  { id: 1, name: "Option1" },
  { id: 2, name: "Option2" },
  { id: 3, name: "Option3" }
]
```

Wait! Again is this state data?

If the list does not change then is not state data. We can start by declaring it as a constant.

```
const options = [
  { id: 1, name: "Option1" },
  { id: 2, name: "Option2" },
  { id: 3, name: "Option3" }
];
```

Let's begin building the radio buttons.

Radion Buttons

When we want to render and manage a list of radio buttons we require a property in the list indicating if the radio button is checked or not.

We are missing this `checked` property in the original array. We may need a list similar to the one below.

```
const newOptions = [
  { id: 1, name: "Option1", checked: false },
  { id: 2, name: "Option2", checked: false },
  { id: 3, name: "Option3", checked: false }
];
```

Can we create the `newOptions` list from the original `options` list?

Yes, we can. Here is a function that takes the original `options` list and creates a new one containing the `checked` property set to be `false`.

```
function uncheckAll(options) {
  return options.map((option) => ({
    ...option,
    checked: false
  }));
}
```

Below the `uncheckAll` function is used to build the `newOptions` list.

```
const newOptions = uncheckAll(options);
```

Here is how we can render such a list on the screen. Notice that the radio button has the type `radio`. In order to display a label near the radio button we need to wrap it inside the `<label>` tag.

```
<form>
  {newOptions.map(({ id, name, checked }) => (
    <label key={id}>
      <input
        type="radio"
        name="options"
        value={id}
        checked={checked}
        onChange={}
      />
      {name}
    </label>
  ))}
</form>
```

Now, let's think about the state data required to render the list of options. Should the option name or id be changed?

No, they don't.

Is there something that does change?

Yes, it is. We need to know if the option is checked or not. The checked property of the option does change. It means that the list of options should be represented as state data.

We define the state associated with the radio list using the useState hook.

```
const [checkedList, setCheckedList] = useState(newOptions);
```

But do we really need the uncheckAll function?

One thing is worth mentioning. When accessing a missing property on an object the result is undefined. undefined is a falsy value.

If we are fine working with the checked property as a boolish value then we don't need the transformation done with the uncheckAll function. In this case, the checked property can be undefined, false, or true.

```
const [checkedList, setCheckedList] = useState(options);
```

checkedList gives access to the current state of the list of options. The setCheckedList allows changing that list.

Now let's think about modifying the checked property of an option inside the list.

When clicking on an option in a radio list the e.target.checked property always returns true. Do not assume that clicking once checks the radio button and clicking again unchecks it. To uncheck a selected radion button click on some other option.

We need a transformation function that checks one option and unchecks all the others.

The following toggleOption function creates a new array where the given id is checked, and all the other options are unchecked.

```
function toggleOption(options, id, checked) {
  return options.map((option) =>
    option.id === id
      ? { ...option, checked }
```

```
      : { ...option, checked: false }
  );
}
```

Why don't we just iterate through all the options and change the `checked` property?

Remember that state data should be treated as immutable. The `map` array method allows us to create a new changed copy of the array having the right `checked` property.

Once we create a new list of options we need to update the state data.

The next `changeList` function modifies the state data. It marks the given `id` as checked and all the other options as unchecked using the `toggleOption` utility function.

```
const changeList = (id, checked) => {
  setCheckedList((checkedList) =>
    toggleOption(checkedList, id, checked));
};
```

Here is the full code for the `RadioList` component.

```
import { useState } from "react";

function RadioList() {
  const [checkedList, setCheckedList] = useState(options);

  const changeList = (id, checked) => {
    setCheckedList((checkedList) =>
      toggleOption(checkedList, id, checked));
  };

  return (
    <form>
    {checkedList.map(({ id, name, checked }) => (
      <label key={id}>
        <input
          type="radio"
          name="options"
          value={id}
          checked={checked}
          onChange={(e) => changeList(id, e.target.checked)}
```

```
      />
      {name}
    </label>
  ))}
  </form>
  );
}
export default RadioList;
```

Checkbox List

Next, let's render and manage the list of checkboxes.

The state associated with the checkbox list is defined in a similar way using the useState hook.

```
const [checkedList, setCheckedList] = useState(options);
```

This time clicking on an option checks it. Clicking again unchecks it.

We need a new function that can toggle the checked property of any option in the list.

The next toggleOption function takes a list of options, an id, and the checked boolean value. It returns a new list of options where the option with the given id is changed. The checked property can be either true or false.

```
function toggleOption(options, id, checked) {
  return options.map((option) =>
    option.id === id ? { ...option, checked } : option
  );
}
```

Below is the changeList function modifying the checked property for the given id in the state using the previous toggleOption function.

```
const changeList = (id, checked) => {
  setCheckedList(checkedList =>
    toggleOption(checkedList, id, checked));
};
```

Here is the full code for the CheckboxList component.

```
function CheckboxList() {
```

```
const [checkedList, setCheckedList] =
  useState(uncheckAll(options));

const changeList = (id, checked) => {
  setCheckedList(checkedList =>
    toggleOption(checkedList, id, checked));
};

return (
  <form>
    {checkedList.map(({ id, name, checked }) => (
      <label key={id}>
        {name}
        <input
          type="checkbox"
          checked={checked}
          onChange={(e) => changeList(id, e.target.checked)}
        />
      </label>
    ))}
  </form>
);
}
export default CheckboxList;
```

Key Notes

- The list of options is state data as the **checked** property changes.
- Remember that the **e.target.checked** property of the change event on a radio button always returns **true** when clicking it. For a checkbox the **e.target.checked** property can be either **true** or **false**.
- When changing the state of an option in a list of radio buttons all the other options should be reset to **false**.
- When changing the state of an option in a checkbox list the other options are not modified.

Chapter 07: Form Validation

Validating the form inputs is a common challenge in most applications. Validating an input usually implies showing an error message somewhere near the associated input.

This chapter shows how to implement a simple validation for a single input text field.

Form

We start by building the form with a single text input and a save button.

```
import { useState } from "react";

function Form() {
  return (
    <form>
      <div>
        <input
          type="text"
          placeholder="name"
        />
      </div>
      <div>
        <button type="button">Save</button>
      </div>
    </form>
  );
}
```

```
export default Form;
```

As already shown we can make the textbox a controlled input by creating an associated state variable and referring to it in the `value` and the `onChange` attributes.

```
import { useState } from "react";

function Form() {
  const [name, setName] = useState("");

  return (
    <form>
      <div>
        <input
          type="text"
          placeholder="name"
          value={name}
          onChange={(e) => setName(e.target.value)}
        />
      </div>
      <div>
        <button type="button">Save</button>
      </div>
    </form>
  );
}

export default Form;
```

Validation Function

A simple name validation may check if the provided text has at least two letters and if the name contains only letters and the "-" character.

The following regular expression verifies just that. The name can only start with a letter.

```
const nameRegEx = /^[a-zA-Z]+[a-zA-Z-]{1,}$/;
```

The `validateName` takes a text and checks if it is a valid name using the previous regular expression.

```
const validateName = (name) => nameRegEx.test(name);
```

At this point the validation function is ready.

Showing the Validation Message

Now we can use the `validateName` function to test if the current name is valid. The result is saved in the `nameIsValid` constant. Each time the text input changes, the `setName` setter function runs and the `Form` function component is invoked. That means the `validateName(name)` runs again and the `nameIsValid` value is recomputed.

```
const nameIsValid = validateName(name);
```

Based on the `nameIsValid` boolean the error is shown below the text input.

```
<form>
  <!--...-->
  {!nameIsValid && (<div>
      Name is invalid
    </div>)}
</form>
```

Errors are usually displayed in red so let's apply a style object to the element containing the validation message.

```
const errorStyle = {
  color: "red"
};
```

The `div` element showing the errors uses the `errorStyle` object.

```
{!nameIsValid && <div style={errorStyle}>Name is invalid</div>}
```

Below is the entire form so far.

```
import { useState } from "react";

const nameRegEx = /^[a-zA-Z]+[a-zA-Z-]{1,}$/;

const validateName = (name) => nameRegEx.test(name);

const errorStyle = {
  color: "red"
```

```
};

function Form() {
  const [name, setName] = useState("");
  const nameIsValid = validateName(name);

  return (
    <form>
      <div>
        <input
          type="text"
          placeholder="name"
          value={name}
          onChange={(e) => setName(e.target.value)}
        />
        {!nameIsValid && (<div style={errorStyle}>
            Name is invalid
          </div>)}
      </div>
      <div>
        <button type="button">Save</button>
      </div>
    </form>
  );
}

export default Form;
```

Validation Message as State

The problem with the previous approach is that the error appears even when the user has not filled in the input and also when the user starts typing. Do we want that?

Not really.

The error messages should not be displayed if the user hasn't started typing. Also, if an error message is displayed, it should be cleared when the user starts typing in the associated input.

What should we do? Does the error message change?

Yes, it does. The error message is empty when first displaying the form.

When the user starts typing the error message is hidden. When the form is submitted the error message is shown if the validation fails.

At this point, we can conclude that the validation result is state data.

```
const [nameIsValid, setNameIsValid] = useState(true);
```

When the form is submitted the validation is triggered and the validation result is saved using the setNameIsValid setter function.

```
const submit = () => {
  const isValid = validateName(name);
  setNameIsValid(isValid);

  if (nameIsValid) {
    console.log("submit");
  }
};
```

Also, when the user starts typing the error message is cleared by setting the name validation to true.

```
const changeName = (newName) => {
  setName(newName);
  setNameIsValid(true);
};
```

The changeName function is set as a handler for the onChange event on the name textbox.

```
<input
  type="text"
  placeholder="name"
  value={name}
  onChange={(e) => changeName(e.target.value)}
/>
```

Showing Several Messages

Storing a boolean validation result allows just a single error message to be displayed.

What if several messages should be displayed for the same input?

In this case, the validation result should not contain a boolean but the error message itself or a code that can be used to detect the entire validation message.

In the next example, the validation function returns the entire message.

```
const validateName = (name) => {
  if (!name.length) return "Name is mandatory";
  if (!nameRegEx.test(name)) return "Name has invalid";
  return;
};
```

When the input value changes the error message should be cleared. We can do this by resetting it to an empty value. An empty string value is a falsy value. This means that it is evaluated to `false` in a boolean context.

```
const changeName = (newName) => {
  setName(newName);
  setNameError("");
};
```

In the `submit` handler the name input is first validated and the new error message is saved. If there is no error then the form can be submitted.

```
const submit = () => {
  const errorMsg = validateName(name);
  setNameError(errorMsg);

  if (!errorMsg) {
    console.log("submit");
  }
};
```

When the error message is empty no error is shown. Otherwise, the error message is displayed on the screen.

```
{nameError && <div style={errorStyle}>{nameError}</div>}
```

Below is the full code for the `Form` component.

```
import { useState } from "react";

const nameRegEx = /^[a-zA-Z]+[a-zA-Z-]{1,}$/;

const validateName = (name) => {
  if (!name.length) return "Name is mandatory";
```

```
    if (!nameRegEx.test(name)) return "Name has invalid";
    return;
};

const errorStyle = {
  color: "red"
};

function Form() {
  const [name, setName] = useState("");
  const [nameError, setNameError] = useState("");

  const changeName = (newName) => {
    setName(newName);
    setNameError("");
  };

  const submit = () => {
    const errorMsg = validateName(name);
    setNameError(errorMsg);

    if (!errorMsg) {
      console.log("submit");
    }
  };

  return (
    <form>
      <div>
        <input
          type="text"
          placeholder="name"
          value={name}
          onChange={(e) => changeName(e.target.value)}
        />
        {nameError && (
          <div style={errorStyle}>{nameError}</div>
        )}
      </div>
      <div>
```

```
      <button type="button" onClick={submit}>
        Save
      </button>
    </div>
  </form>
 );
}


export default Form;
```

Key Notes

- When the form is displayed no error messages are shown. When the form is submitted the input fields are validated and the related error messages are displayed.
- An error message can change and as such, it is stored as state data.
- There may be several error messages for a single input so it is a good idea to store the error message text or an error code.
- The error message is shown below the related input using conditional rendering.

Chapter 08: Form Validation Custom Hook

In the previous chapter, we wrote the validation logic for a single input. Next, we take that logic and extract it out in a custom hook. Once the hook is ready we can use it to validate several inputs in a form.

State Form Hook

Let's first remember the `useForm` hook used to handle the state for several fields.

```
import { useState } from "react";

function useForm(fields) {
  const [state, setState] = useState(fields);

  const setField = (e) => {
    const name = e.target.name;
    const value =
      e.target.type === "checkbox"
        ? e.target.checked
        : e.target.value;

    setState((prevState) =>
      ({ ...prevState, [name]: value }));
  };

  return [state, setField];
}
```

```
export default useForm;
```

At the moment it takes a single object with all the inputs to manage and their initial value.

```
import useForm from "./useForm";

function LoginForm() {
  const [state, setField] = useForm({
    username: "",
    password: "",
    rememberMe: false
  });

  const submit = () => {}
  return ();
}


export default LoginForm;
```

Validation Hook

If we want to validate those fields we need some extra validation information. Let's start by adding a new parameter taking the validations for all fields.

```
function useForm(fields, validations) {}
```

To make things clearer we are going to rename the state variable storing the input values to values.

We need also a state variable (errors) storing all the error messages. A validation function that checks all the input fields and updates the error state variable is required.

```
import { useState } from "react";

function useForm(fields, validations) {
  const [values, setValues] = useState(fields);
  const [errors, setErrors] = useState({});

  const setField = (e) => {}

  const validate = () => {
```

```
      return false;
  };

  return { values, errors, setField, validate };
}
```

```
export default useForm;
```

Now the custom hook exports the **errors** object containing all the validation messages and the **validate** function validating all the form inputs.

A validation object describing how to validate a field may look like the one below. In this example, the **name** field is required and it has to match the regular expression specified in the **pattern** property.

```
{
  name: {
    required: true,
    pattern: nameRegEx
  }
}
```

We can write a function that uses such an object and validates the value for a single input. The **name** parameter is required for creating the validation error message.

```
const validateValue = (value, name, validation) => {
  if (validation.required && !value.length){
    return `${name} is mandatory`;
  }

  if (validation.pattern && !validation.pattern.test(value)){
    return `${name} has invalid`;
  }

  return;
};
```

At this point, we can make a new validation setter function that extracts the value to be validated from the **values** state variable and then uses the previous function, **validateValue**, to test it. Once the value is validated the associated error message is updated.

```
const validateFieldByName = (name) => {
```

```
const value = values[name];
const validation = validations[name];
const errorMsg = validateValue(value, name, validation);
setErrors((prevState) =>
  ({ ...prevState, [name]: errorMsg }));
return !errorMsg;
};
```

The `validate` function is the one validating all the fields. If any of the input validation fails then the form is invalid.

```
const validate = () => {
  const fieldNames = Object.keys(fields);
  const validationResults = fieldNames.map(validateFieldByName)
  const hasError = validationResults.includes(false);
  return !hasError;
};
```

All the fields' names are already available as properties on the `fields` input parameter. The `Object.keys` utility is used to get the fields' names as an array of names. The `map` array method calls `validateFieldByName` for each field and gets the result as an array of booleans. This array is stored in the `validationResults` constant.

We may also need to clear the associated error message once the user starts typing in an input.

```
const setField = (e) => {
  //...
  setErrors((prevState) => ({ ...prevState, [name]: "" }));
};
```

That is basically all we have to do for adding a simple validation system to the `useForm` hook. Below you can check what the structure of the custom hook looks like.

```
import { useState } from "react";

const validateValue = (value, name, validation) => {}

function useForm(fields, validations) {
  const [values, setValues] = useState(fields);
  const [errors, setErrors] = useState({});
```

```
  const setField = (e) => {}
  const validateFieldByName = (name) => {}
  const validate = () => {}

  return { values, errors, setField, validate };
}


export default useForm;
```

Validating a Single Input

Now that the custom hook is ready let's use it to validate a single name input. Below you can check how the two data variables(`values` and `errors`) and the two functions (`setField` and `validate`) are extracted from the custom hook.

```
import useForm from "./useForm";

const nameRegEx = /^[a-zA-Z]+[a-zA-Z-]{1,}$/;

function Form() {
  const { values, errors, setField, validate } = useForm(
    {
      name: ""
    },
    {
      name: {
        required: true,
        pattern: nameRegEx
      }
    }
  );

  return (
    <form></form>
  );
}


export default Form;
```

The `validate` function can then be used in the `submit` handler. It validates all the fields and returns a boolean. If the form is valid the data can then be submitted.

```
const submit = () => {
  const isvalid = validate();

  if (isvalid) {
    console.log(values);
  }
};
```

If there is an error message for the **name** field then this message is displayed below the input.

```
function Form() {
  //...

  return (
    <form>
      <div>
        <input
          type="text"
          name="name"
          value={values.name}
          onChange={setField}
        />
        {errors.name && (
          <div style={errorStyle}>
            {errors.name}
          </div>
        )}
      </div>
      <!-- ... -->
    </form>
  );
}
```

```
export default Form;
```

Validating Several Inputs

Next, let's use the custom hook to validate several inputs. Because the logic for rendering an input and the associated error message is repeated we can extract it from the component and reuse it several times.

Here is the Input component taking all the necessary data and rendering both the input and the associated error.

```
const errorStyle = {
  color: "red"
};

function Input({ value, name, label, error, onChange }) {
  return (
    <>
      <input
        placeholder={label || name}
        type="text"
        name={name}
        value={value}
        onChange={onChange}
      />
      {error && <div style={errorStyle}>{error}</div>}
    </>
  );
}
```

```
export default Input;
```

Next, we build a form with three inputs like the one below.

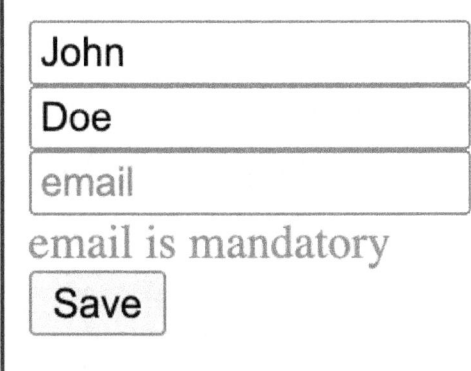

Below is the full form.

```
import useForm from "./useForm";
import Input from "./Input";

const nameRegEx = /^[a-zA-Z]+[a-zA-Z-]{1,}$/;
const emailRegEx = /^(.+)@(.+)$/;

function Form() {
  const { values, errors, setField, validate } = useForm(
    {
      fname: "",
      lname: "",
      email: ""
    },
    {
      fname: {
        required: true,
        pattern: nameRegEx
      },
      lname: {
        required: true,
        pattern: nameRegEx
      },
      email: {
        required: true,
        pattern: emailRegEx
      }
    }
  );

  const submit = () => {
    const isvalid = validate();

    if (isvalid) {
      console.log(values);
    }
  };

  return (
    <form>
      <div>
```

```
        <Input
          name="fname"
          label="first name"
          value={values.fname}
          error={errors.fname}
          onChange={setField}
        />
      </div>
      <div>
        <Input
          name="lname"
          label="last name"
          value={values.lname}
          error={errors.lname}
          onChange={setField}
        />
      </div>
      <div>
        <Input
          name="email"
          value={values.email}
          error={errors.email}
          onChange={setField}
        />
      </div>
      <div>
        <button type="button" onClick={submit}>
          Save
        </button>
      </div>
    </form>
  );
}


export default Form;
```

Key Notes

- Storing the error messages for several fields requires a state object with a property for each associated input.
- The validation logic can be encapsulated in a custom hook that

gets an object describing the form fields and the required validation. This hook gives access to an **errors** object containing the error for each field and a function that validates all the inputs.

Chapter 09: Adding and Deleting Items in Lists

Next, we create a simple Todo application and analyze the state involved in such functionality. The application allows the user to add a new todo and delete an existing one.

List

Let's first define the `TodoList` component that renders all the todos. The list component just takes a list of todos and maps each object into a list item element.

```
function TodoList({ todos }) {
  return (
    <ul>
      {todos.map((todo) => (
        <li>{todo.name}</li>
      ))}
    </ul>
  );
}
```

```
export default TodoList;
```

The todo object is mapped to the `<li>{todo.name}</li>` element and all the `<li>` elements are wrapped inside the `<ul>` element.

Form

In order to add a new todo, a form is needed. The form contains single input asking for a name.

Do we need state data for that input?

Yes, we do.

```
const [name, setName] = useState("");
```

The name input is a controlled input. It has an associated state value and both `value` and `onChange` attributes are referring to that.

Here is the form component.

```
import { useState } from "react";

function TodoForm({ onAdd }) {
  const [name, setName] = useState("");

  return (
    <form>
      <input
        type="text"
        value={name}
        onChange={(e) => setName(e.target.value)}
      />
      <button type="button">
        Add
      </button>
    </form>
  );
}

export default TodoForm;
```

We need a way to allow parent components to access the new todo name when the save button is clicked.

How can we do that?

Remember that function components can receive primitives or objects as inputs, but they call also receive functions.

In order to communicate with parent components we can receive callback functions as input. Later we can invoke these callback functions with the data we want to send to the parent components.

Here is the `Form` component receiving the `onAdd` callback.

```
function TodoForm({ onAdd }) {}
```

Ok, what should we do next? When this **onAdd** callback function should be called?

One place to call it is when the add button is clicked. First, we need to define such a handler function.

```
const submit = () => {}
```

Then we assign the **submit** function as the handler for the click event on the add button.

```
<button type="button" onClick={submit}>
  Add
</button>
```

The **submit** handler invokes the **onAdd** callback with the new todo name.

```
const submit = () => {
  if (onAdd) onAdd(name);
};
```

One other thing we can do is clear the name once the add button is clicked. We can do that by setting the name to an empty string in the submit handler.

```
const submit = () => {
  if (onAdd) onAdd(name);
  setName("");
};
```

Below is the full **Form** component.

```
import { useState } from "react";

function TodoForm({ onAdd }) {
  const [name, setName] = useState("");

  const submit = () => {
    if (onAdd) onAdd(name);
    setName("");
  };

  return (
    <form>
```

66

```
      <input
        type="text"
        value={name}
        onChange={(e) => setName(e.target.value)}
      />
      <button type="button" onClick={submit}>
        Add
      </button>
    </form>
  );
}

export default TodoForm;
```

Showing the List

At this point, we can use the previous components to render a hardcoded list of todos.

Here is a list of todos with two items.

```
const initialTodos = [
  { id: 1, name: "clean house" },
  { id: 2, name: "do shopping" }
];
```

Again how can we render this on the screen?

Indeed, simply by passing this information to the TodoList component. It will display it.

```
import TodoList from "./TodoList";

function App() {
  return (
    <div>
      <TodoList todos={initialTodos} />
    </div>
  );
}

export default App;
```

The TodoForm component can be shown above the list component.

```
import TodoForm from "./TodoForm";
import TodoList from "./TodoList";

function App() {
  return (
    <div>
      <TodoForm />
      <TodoList todos={initialTodos} />
    </div>
  );
}

export default App;
```

Adding a Todo

Ok. We managed to define and render a hardcoded list of data. Next, we will add a new todo to that list.

What does it mean to add a new todo to the list?

It means that the list data should change. It implies that the list data should be stored as state.

```
const [list, setList] = useState(initialTodos);
```

How do we know in the App component that the add button was clicked in its child form component?

We need to define a handler for the onAdd event of the Form component. We can call the handler with the same name as the event, addTodo.

```
const addTodo = (name) => {};
```

```
//...
<TodoForm onAdd={addTodo} />
```

Ok. What should we do now in the add handler?

First, we need to create a new todo. What are the properties of a todo?

Yes, name and id. We already have the name, we just have to generate a new id on the fly. We can use the Date.now() function. It returns a new number each it is called. It returns the number of milliseconds since the beginning of January 1, 1970.

```
const addTodo = (name) => {
const todo = {
  id: Date.now(),
    name
  };
};
```

How can we add it to the existing list?

Remember that state data should be treated as immutable. We can not use the **push** array method. That changes the current array. One option is to create a new copy of the array using the spread operator ([...list]) and then add the new todo at the end.

```
const newList = [...list, todo];
```

Once the **newList** containing the new todo is ready we can update the state data.

```
const addTodo = (name) => {
const todo = {
  id: Date.now(),
    name
  };
  const newList = [...list, todo];
  setList(newList);
};
```

Here is the full component so far.

```
import { useState } from "react";
import TodoForm from "./TodoForm";
import TodoList from "./TodoList";

const initialTodos = [
  { id: 1, name: "clean house" },
  { id: 2, name: "do shopping" }
];

function App() {
  const [list, setList] = useState(initialTodos);

  const addTodo = (name) => {
    const todo = {
```

```
      id: Date.now(),
      name
    };
    const newList = [...list, todo];
    setList(newList);
  };

  return (
    <div>
      <TodoForm onAdd={addTodo} />
      <TodoList todos={list} />
    </div>
  );
}

export default App;
```

Deleting a Todo

Next, let's focus on deleting a todo from the list.

In what component does the delete happen?

The deletion occurs in the list component.

How can we communicate that a todo was deleted in a child component to the parent **App** component?

We can do it in a similar to what we did for the addition. First, we add a new callback function (**onDelete**) as input to the list component.

```
function TodoList({ todos, onDelete }) {}
```

We also need to add a delete button on each list item. Let's do that.

```
function TodoList({ todos, onDelete }) {
  return (
    <ul>
      {todos.map((todo) => (
        <li>
          {todo.name} 
          <button onClick={() => {}}>
            Delete
          </button>
```

```
        </li>
      ))}
    </ul>
  );
}
```

When the delete button is clicked the `onDelete` callback is called with the id of the current todo. The id of the todo is enough for deleting it from the list.

```
function TodoList({ todos, onDelete }) {
  return (
    <ul>
      {todos.map((todo) => (
        <li>
          {todo.name} 
          <button
            onClick={() => {
              if (onDelete) onDelete(todo.id);
            }}
          >
            Delete
          </button>
        </li>
      ))}
    </ul>
  );
}
```

```
export default TodoList;
```

At this point, the `TodoList` component exposes the `onDelete` event.

What else do we have to do to actually delete the item from the list?

We need a handler for `deleteTodo` event. Let it have the same name.

```
const deleteTodo = (id) => {};
```

```
//..
```

```
<TodoList todos={list} onDelete={deleteTodo} />
```

Now let's think about implementing the delete handler. We should treat the state data as being immutable so we can use the `filter` array method to create a new array without the specified id.

```
const newList = list.filter((todo) => todo.id !== id);
```

Once we have the new list we update the state data.

```
const deleteTodo = (id) => {
  const newList = list.filter((todo) => todo.id !== id);
  setList(newList);
};
```

That was all. Here is the full code for `App` component.

```
import { useState } from "react";
import TodoForm from "./TodoForm";
import TodoList from "./TodoList";

const initialTodos = [
  { id: 1, name: "clean house" },
  { id: 2, name: "do shopping" }
];

function App() {
  const [list, setList] = useState(initialTodos);

  const addTodo = (name) => {
    const todo = {
      id: Date.now(),
      name
    };
    const newList = [...list, todo];
    setList(newList);
  };

  const deleteTodo = (id) => {
    const newList = list.filter((todo) => todo.id !== id);
    setList(newList);
  };

  return (
    <div>
      <TodoForm onAdd={addTodo} />
```

```
        <TodoList todos={list} onDelete={deleteTodo} />
      </div>
  );
}

export default App;
```

Key Notes

- Adding or deleting items means changing the list data. The list should be stored as state data.
- Adding an item to the list can be done by cloning the current array using the spread operator and adding the new element.
- Deleting an item from the list may be done by using the `filter` array method.
- In order to communicate with parent components, the child components can receive callback functions as input. These callbacks are invoked inside the child component with the right data.

Chapter 10: Refactoring with the Reducer Hook

There is also another hook for defining the state in the function component. This is the reducer hook. Next, we discuss it and then refactor the previous Todo application using it.

Reducer Hook

Let's start by introducing the reducer hook.

The reducer hook defines the state in a function component, similar to the state hook. It takes a slightly different approach and gets a reducer function as input besides the initial state value.

The important part to discuss here is the reducer function.

The reducer is a function taking two parameters, the current state and an action. It transforms the current state and returns a new state. State and action can be of any type, but actions are usually objects having the `type` and the `payload` properties.

The reducer is a pure function.

The reducer hook returns a state variable and a dispatch function. The state variable allows us to read the state. The dispatch function lets us changes that state by dispatching actions.

```
const [state, dispatch] = useReducer(reducer, initialState);
```

Things will become more clear once we start refactoring the Todo app.

Creating the Reducer

Let's refactor the app using the reducer hook.

First, we need to create the reducer function. It takes the current state data and an action. The state in our case is the list of todos.

```
function todosReducer(list, action) {}
```

What are our actions for the Todo app? What the user can actually do?

There are basically two actions the user can do, adding and deleting a todo. Let's call these add_todo and delete_todo. Below is an example of a delete action object.

```
{
  type: "delete_todo",
  payload: 1
}
```

Here is an example of an add action object.

```
{
  type: "add_todo",
  payload: "do the laundry"
}
```

The reducer function should handle these two actions.

When the add_todo action is received a new list containing the new todo is returned. When the delete_todo action is received a new list without the given todo is returned. When anything else is received the state remains the same.

We already have two functions, addTodo and deleteTodo, changing the list.

```
function addTodo(list, name) {
  const todo = {
    id: Date.now(),
    name
  };
  const newList = [...list, todo];
  return newList;
}
```

```
function deleteTodo(list, id) {
  const newList = list.filter((todo) => todo.id !== id);
  return newList;
}
```

We just need to map these two functions to the matching action types. Here is how we can do that inside the reducer.

```
function todosReducer(list, action) {
  switch (action.type) {
    case "add_todo":
      return addTodo(list, action.payload);
    case "delete_todo":
      return deleteTodo(list, action.payload);
    default:
      return list;
  }
}
```

Using the Reducer

Now let's use the reducer hook to create a state variable.

```
const [list, dispatch] =
  useReducer(todosReducer, initialTodos);
```

list is a state variable. It can be changed by dispatching actions using the dispatch function. At this moment it supports only the add_todo and delete_todo actions. Dispatching other actions does not change the existing list.

We may also create two additional functions for adding and deleting a todo. They are just calling the dispatch function.

```
const addTodo = (name) => {
  dispatch({ type: "add_todo", payload: name });
};

const deleteTodo = (id) => {
  dispatch({ type: "delete_todo", payload: id });
};
```

The new functions can then be used as handlers for the onAdd and onDelete events.

```
<TodoForm onAdd={addTodo} />
<TodoList todos={list} onDelete={deleteTodo} />
```

Here is the **App** component using the reducer hook to define the internal state.

```
import { useReducer } from "react";
import TodoForm from "./TodoForm";
import TodoList from "./TodoList";

const initialTodos = [];

function addTodo(list, name) {}

function deleteTodo(list, id) {}

function todosReducer(list, action) {
  switch (action.type) {
    case "add_todo":
      return addTodo(list, action.payload);
    case "delete_todo":
      return deleteTodo(list, action.payload);
    default:
      return list;
  }
}

function App() {
  const [list, dispatch] =
    useReducer(todosReducer, initialTodos);

  const addTodo = (name) => {
    dispatch({ type: "add_todo", payload: name });
  };

  const deleteTodo = (id) => {
    dispatch({ type: "delete_todo", payload: id });
  };

  return (
    <div>
```

```
      <TodoForm onAdd={addTodo} />
      <TodoList todos={list} onDelete={deleteTodo} />
    </div>
  );
}

export default App;
```

Reducer by Convention

We can simplify the reducer creation by using a convention. The convention can be to have the same name for both the action and the associated function handling it.

In our case, the `addTodo` function handles the add and the `deleteTodo` function handles the delete.

```
const todosReducer = createReducer([addTodo, deleteTodo]);
```

`addTodo` is now the type of the add action, and `deleteTodo` is the type of the delete action.

Here is a helper function making a reducer by convention. It gets an array of smaller functions computing the new state.

```
function createReducer(reducers) {
  return function (state, action) {
    const reducer =
      reducers.find((r) => r.name === action.type);

    return reducer(state, action.payload) ?? state;
  };
}
```

The `reducers` input is an array of mini reducer functions. It can be something like `[addTodo, deleteTodo]`. The `find` array method is used to detect the associated mini reducer for an action. For example, for the action with the type `addTodo` the associated mini-reducer is `addTodo`. When no such mini reducer is found the state remains unchanged. When the mini reducer is found, then it is called with the current state and the received action. The result computed by the mini reducer is returned.

We can extract the reducer logic in its own file, and use it inside the component.

```
const initialTodos = [
  { id: 1, name: "clean house" },
  { id: 2, name: "do shopping" }
];

function addTodo(list, name) {
  const todo = {
    id: Date.now(),
    name
  };
  const newList = [...list, todo];
  return newList;
}

function deleteTodo(list, id) {
  const newList = list.filter((todo) => todo.id !== id);
  return newList;
}

function createReducer(reducers) {
  return function (state, action) {
    const reducer =
      reducers.find((r) => r.name === action.type);

    return reducer(state, action.payload) ?? state;
  };
}

const todosReducer = createReducer([addTodo, deleteTodo]);

export { initialTodos, addTodo, deleteTodo };
export default todosReducer;
```

Here is the full **App** component creating a reducer by convention and then using it to manage the internal state.

```
import { useReducer } from "react";
import TodoForm from "./TodoForm";
import TodoList from "./TodoList";
import todosReducer, { initialTodos } from "./reducer";
```

```
function App() {
  const [list, dispatch] =
    useReducer(todosReducer, initialTodos);

  const addTodo = (name) => {
    dispatch({ type: "addTodo", payload: name });
  };

  const deleteTodo = (id) => {
    dispatch({ type: "deleteTodo", payload: id });
  };

  return (
    <div>
      <TodoForm onAdd={addTodo} />
      <TodoList todos={list} onDelete={deleteTodo} />
    </div>
  );
}

export default App;
```

Key Notes

- The reducer hook allows defining state inside a function component. It takes a reducer function and the initial state.
- The reducer function gets the current state and an action and returns the new state.
- Transforming the state is done by dispatching actions
- Actions are usually plain objects having the `type` and the `payload` properties.
- In a way, the reducer hook guides us to extract the state management logic outside the component in a new function called reducer.

Chapter 11: Master Detail

Next, we discuss state management in a master-detail interface.

We start displaying a list of items, and when one is selected we show its details. Then we allow editing its contents. It is a simple scenario but has a few challenges.

Details Component

First, we need a new component displaying the details of the selected item. Initially, these details are read-only.

The `DetailsView` component takes the selected item and displays its information inside a `<div>` element.

```
function DetailsView({ item }) {
  return (
    <div>
      <div>{item.id}</div>
      <div>{item.name}</div>
    </div>
  );
}

export default DetailsView;
```

Rendering the List

Creating a list component is also straightforward. Consider a list of items like the one below.

```
[
  { id: 1, name: "Radio" },
```

```
  { id: 2, name: "Headset" },
  { id: 3, name: "Keyboard" }
]
```

How can we render such a list?

We can simply map the list of items to `<div>` elements.

```
function List({ items}) {
  return (
    <div>
      {items.map((item) => (
        <div key={item.id}>
          <div>{item.name}</div>
          <div>
            <button type="button">
              Select
            </button>
          </div>
        </div>
      ))}
    </div>
  );
}
```

```
export default List;
```

Now let's think about the events of the list component. What should happen when the user clicks on an item?

The `onClick` event should be exposed to the parent components.

Let's take the `onClick` callback as input.

```
function DetailsView({ item, onClick }) {}
```

Then when the user clicks the select button the `onClick` callback is invoked with the selected item.

```
<button type="button" onClick={() => onClick(item)}>
  Select
</button>
```

By handling the `onClick` event, the parent component is notified when an item is selected and has access to that item.

Selecting an Item

The `App` component is the parent component rendering the list using the `List` component and showing the `Details` component when one item is selected.

Let's start by rendering the initial list of items using the `List` component.

```
import { useState } from "react";
import List from "./List";

const initialList = [
  { id: 1, name: "Radio" },
  { id: 2, name: "Headset" },
  { id: 3, name: "Keyboard" }
];

function App() {
  return (
    <div>
      <List items={initialList} />
    </div>
  );
}
export default App;
```

Next, we need to be able to select an item. What does it actually mean?

Remember that the UI should be a reflection of state data.

Initially, there is no selected item. Once the user clicks on an item the selected item changes. The selected item needs to be represented as state data.

```
const [selectedItem, setSelectedItem] = useState(null);
```

The `Details` component should be displayed only when there is a selected item. The `selectedItem` should be sent to the `Details` component.

```
{selectedItem && <Details item={selectedItem} />}
```

When the user clicks on an item the selected item should be changed.

```
<List items={initialList} onClick={setSelectedItem} />
```

What about the list of items? Does it change?

At the moment, we just display the list of items so it does not change. We don't need to store it as state data. Below is the full **App** component.

```
import { useState } from "react";
import List from "./List";
import Details from "./DetailsView";

const initialList = [
  { id: 1, name: "Radio" },
  { id: 2, name: "Headset" },
  { id: 3, name: "Keyboard" }
];

function App() {
  const [selectedItem, setSelectedItem] = useState(null);

  return (
    <div>
      <List items={initialList} onClick={setSelectedItem} />

      {selectedItem && (
        <Details
          item={selectedItem} />
      )}
    </div>
  );
}

export default App;
```

Editing an Item

Everything went well so far. Now let's allow editing of the selected item.

This time we need a form. Below is one containing a text input for editing the name and a save button.

```
function DetailsEdit({ item }) {
  return (
    <form>
      <div>{item.id}</div>
      <div>
```

```
            <input type="text" />
          </div>
          <div>
            <button type="button" onClick={save}>
              Save
            </button>
          </div>
        </form>
    );
}
export default DetailsEdit;
```

Is there any state data need for this form? Remember what was discussed about controlled inputs.

We need a state variable that is associated with the name input.

```
import { useState } from "react";

function DetailsEdit({ item }) {
  const [name, setName] = useState(item.name);

  return (
    <form>
      <div>{item.id}</div>
      <div>
        <input
          type="text"
          value={name}
          onChange={(e) => setName(e.target.value)}
        />
      </div>
      <div>
        <button type="button">
          Save
        </button>
      </div>
    </form>
  );
}
export default DetailsEdit;
```

Ok, what about the external components? How do they know when the save button has been pressed?

We need a callback input in the details component. It can be named onSave.

```
function DetailsEdit({ item, onSave }) {}
```

When invoking the onSave callback we should pass the new item object. Let's do that in a new save handler.

```
const save = () => {
  const newItem = {
    id: item.id,
    name
  };
  onSave(newItem);
};
```

```
//...
<button type="button" onClick={save}>
  Save
</button>
```

Below is the details form component so far.

```
import { useEffect, useState } from "react";

function DetailsEdit({ item, onSave }) {
  const [name, setName] = useState(item.name);

  const save = () => {
    const newItem = {
      id: item.id,
      name
    };
    onSave(newItem);
  };

  return (
    <form>
      <div>{item.id}</div>
      <div>
```

```
    <input
      type="text"
      value={name}
      onChange={(e) => setName(e.target.value)}
    />
  </div>
  <div>
    <button type="button" onClick={save}>
      Save
    </button>
  </div>
</form>
  );
}
```

```
export default DetailsEdit;
```

Let's test it. Is everything working ok?

When we test the current behavior of the details component we can notice that the form is loaded correctly only the first time. After that, when selecting new items, the name is not refreshing only the id does.

Why is that?

The name state variable is associated with the name input. The input shows what is in that variable. The **name** variable does not update automatically when selecting a new item.

When selecting a new item the **item** parameter is updated but the **name**state variable is not. The solution is to update the state when the input parameter changes.

How can we do that?

The effect hook solves this challenge. It allows us to run a callback when its dependency array changes. So we can create a dependency array containing the item parameter. Here is what it looks like.

```
useEffect(() => {
  setName(item.name);
}, [item]);
```

When the **item** input parameter changes, the **setName** setter function is invoked and updates the state variable.

Below is the form details component.

```
import { useEffect, useState } from "react";

function DetailsEdit({ item, onSave }) {
  const [name, setName] = useState(item.name);

  useEffect(() => {
    setName(item.name);
  }, [item]);

  const save = () => {
    const newItem = {
      id: item.id,
      name
    };
    onSave(newItem);
  };

  return (
    <form>
      <div>{item.id}</div>
      <div>
        <input
          type="text"
          value={name}
          onChange={(e) => setName(e.target.value)}
        />
      </div>
      <div>
        <button type="button" onClick={save}>
          Save
        </button>
      </div>
    </form>
  );
}

export default DetailsEdit;
```

Editing Items in the List

Now that the details component allows us to edit an item, let's use it inside the **App** component.

We should update the list of items with the new one. Now, the list of items does change so it should be declared as state data.

```
const [items, setItems] = useState(initialList);
```

We need a new handler for the **onSave** event.

```
const save = (newItem) => {}
```

```
//...
<Details item={selectedItem} onSave={save} />
```

What else do we need to do?

Here is a function that takes a list and the new item and returns a new list where the given item is updated.

```
function editItem(list, newItem) {
  return list.map((item) =>
    (item.id === newItem.id ? newItem : item));
}
```

In the **save** handler function we use the previous function to get the newly updated list. The new list is provided to the **setItems** setter function. In the same handler, we can also hide the details form by setting the selected item to **null**.

```
const save = (newItem) => {
  setItems((list) => editItem(list, newItem));
  setSelectedItem(null);
};
```

Finally here is the full code for the **App** component.

```
import { useState } from "react";
import List from "./List";
import Details from "./DetailsEdit";

function editItem(list, newItem) {
  return list.map((item) =>
    (item.id === newItem.id ? newItem : item));
```

```
}

const initialList = [
  { id: 1, name: "Radio" },
  { id: 2, name: "Headset" },
  { id: 3, name: "Keyboard" }
];

function App() {
  const [items, setItems] = useState(initialList);
  const [selectedItem, setSelectedItem] = useState(null);

  const save = (newItem) => {
    setItems((list) => editItem(list, newItem));
    setSelectedItem(null);
  };

  return (
    <div>
      <List items={items} onClick={setSelectedItem} />
      {selectedItem && (
        <Details
          item={selectedItem}
          onSave={save} />
      )}
    </div>
  );
}

export default App;
```

Key Notes

- When the list of data changes it should become state data.
- The selected item changes and should be declared as state data.
- When state data depends on the input parameters we need to detect when those parameters change using the effect hook and update the state with the new values.

Chapter 12: Timers

This chapter looks at the challenge of reading the current state inside timers.

There are two types of timers we can create in JavaScript. One is the timeout timer. It runs once after a specified amount of time. It is built using the `setTimeout` utility function.

The other is the interval timer created with the `setInterval` utility function. It runs at the given interval.

Accessing the state in both these timers has challenges.

A Simple Counter

Let's start by creating a simple `Counter` component. It displays a counter and a button incrementing its value.

Here is the markup for it.

```
function Counter() {
  return (
    <div>
      {count}
      <button
      onClick={}>
        Increment
      </button>
    </div>
  );
}
export default Counter;
```

Let's think about the state data required for such functionality.

Is there something that does changes? Yes, it is. The counter changes. It is incremented when the user clicks on the increment button. The counter values should be stored as state data.

```
const [count, setCount] = useState(0);
```

Below is the full **Counter**component. When the increment button is clicked the **setCount** setter function is called. It gets the **increment**updater function.

increment is a simple function that increments a given number.

```
import { useState } from "react";

function increment(n) {
  return n + 1;
}

function Counter() {
  const [count, setCount] = useState(0);

  return (
    <div>
      {count}
      <button
       onClick={() => setCount(increment)}>
         Increment
      </button>
    </div>
  );
}

export default Counter;
```

Timeout Timer

Next, let's try to display the state value after five seconds.

As said we can use the timeout timer to run a callback function after the given amount of milliseconds.

```
setTimeout(() => {}, 5000);
```

So we can simply invoke the `setTimeout` utility to show the count value after five seconds.

```
import { useState } from "react";

function Counter() {
  const [count, setCount] = useState(0);

  setTimeout(() => {
    console.log(count);
  }, 5000);

  return ();
}

export default Counter;
```

Now let's check what happens.

Click the increment button twice and then wait five seconds. The value logged in the console should be 2. Nonetheless, if we look in the console we see three logs.

```
//0 after 5 seconds
//1
//2
```

Why is this happening? Why are three logs created instead of one?

Each time we press the increment button, the function component is executed and it starts a new timer. Each new timer displays the new incremented value after five seconds.

One timer is started when the component is rendered. The other two clicks start two additional timers. In total three timers are started and they display three logs in the console.

Starting a Single Timer

We should not start a new timeout timer when clicking the increment button. A single timer should be started when the component is first rendered.

Executing a piece of logic only when the component is rendered can be achieved using the effect hook. Passing an empty array as a dependency to the effect hook allows us to run the callback only after the first render.

```
useEffect(() => {}, [])
```

We just have to make the `setTimeout` call inside the callback for the effect hook.

```
import { useEffect, useState } from "react";

function Counter() {
  const [count, setCount] = useState(0);

  useEffect(() => {
    setTimeout(() => {
      console.log(count);
    }, 2000);
  }, []);

  return ();
}

export default Counter;
```

Things are better now. Even if we click the increment button twice, we find only one log in the console. The problem is that it has the wrong value. It displays 0.

If we had clicked the increment button twice before the callback ran, the value recorded in the console should be 2.

Why is the value in the console 0 instead of 2?

When the `setTimeout` is invoked, the inline callback passed as input is actually a closure function pointing to the value of the counter at the creation time. This means that the count value inside the closure function is 0 no matter how many times we change the count value.

Ref Hook

One way to access the current value of the state data inside the closure function is to create the closure around a reference object. The closure function always points to the same object but the actual value stored by the object changes every time the `Counter` function runs.

We can get a reference to the same object every time the function component runs using the **useRef** hook.

```
const countRef = useRef(count);
```

The **useRef** hook returns a mutable ref object having the **current** property. The **current** property gets initialized with the given argument.

The **useRef** hook creates a plain object but it gives the same ref object on every render. The important part here is that we are dealing with the same object on all re-renders. Creating an object with the object liters syntax {current: count} makes a new object on every re-render.

Every time the function component runs the **current** property of this object is updated. Changing the **current** property does not trigger a re-render.

```
countRef.current = count;
```

Now in the timeout callback the **countRef.current** points to the current state value.

```
useEffect(() => {
  setTimeout(() => {
    console.log(countRef.current);
  }, 5000);
}, []);
```

Here is the full code showing the current value of the state when the timeout callback runs.

```
import { useEffect, useRef, useState } from "react";

function increment(n) {
  return n + 1;
}

function Counter() {
  const [count, setCount] = useState(0);
  const countRef = useRef();
  countRef.current = count;

  useEffect(() => {
    setTimeout(() => {
      console.log(countRef.current);
```

```
      }, 5000);
    }, []);

    return (
      <div>
        {count}
        <button
         onClick={() => setCount(increment)}>
          Increment
        </button>
      </div>
    );
}
```

```
export default Counter;
```

Using an Updater Function

We have arrived at this complicated solution because we wanted to read the current state value in a timer callback. When we just want to access the current state to change it things are much simpler. We just have to use the setter function (setCount) and provide an updater callback. The updater callback provides access to the latest state value.

Let's say that after five seconds we want to increase the current counter by 100.

The following code gets the wrong current counter value.

```
useEffect(() => {
  setTimeout(() => {
    console.log(count);
    setCount(count + 100);
  }, 5000);
}, []);
```

The best practice is to use an updater function when changing the state value as it always gets access to the current state value. Check the code below.

```
useEffect(() => {
  setTimeout(() => {
    setCount((count) => count + 100);
```

```
  }, 5000);
}, []);
```

The updater function acquires the current state as input and returns the new state.

Digital Clock

Next, we will create a simple digital clock.

Let's think about it. What do we need in order to create such a clock?

Ok. So first we require a way to get the current time. Then what's next?

We basically need to get the current time every second and display it on the screen and that implies the use of a timer.

Current Time

Let's start by getting the current time.

The **Date** constructor function creates an object storing the current date and time. The next function gives such a date object.

```
function now(){
  return new Date();
}
```

Once we have this object we can extract the current time as a string.

```
const currentDateTime = new Date();
const timeText = currentDateTime.toLocaleTimeString();
```

The **toLocaleTimeString** method returns a localized string representation of the time portion of the date.

Clock Component

At this point, we know how to detect the current time.

How can we display the time-formatted string in a function component?

Below is an example of a component creating a **Date** object and rendering the time.

```
function Clock(){
  const date = new Date();
```

```
  return (
    <span>
      {date.toLocaleTimeString()}
    </span>
  );
}
```

```
export default Clock;
```

This component displays the time when it is rendered on the screen. After that nothing happens. The time is not updated.

What does it mean to update the time?

Updating the time on the screen means changing the associated state data.

State

Let's start by transforming the current time from a simple variable into state data. For this, we use the **useState** hook.

```
const [date, setDate] = useState(new Date());
```

Now how can we change the current time using the **setDate** setter function?

Below is an example of a function (**refreshClock**) changing the state date object with a new one storing the current date and time.

```
function refreshClock() {
  setDate(new Date());
}
```

Interval Timer

At this point, we have the current date and time as state in the Clock component. We just need to change it at the right moment and the new time will be displayed on the screen.

The **setInterval** utility function calls the provided callback function at the specified intervals (in milliseconds). The timer created by the **setInterval** utility runs until the **clearInterval** utility function is called. The id value returned by `setInterval` is used as the argument for the `clearInterval` function.

Basically, we need to create new `Date` objects every second.

```
const timerId = setInterval(refreshClock, 1000);
```

If we leave the code like this, every re-render of the component creates a new interval timer. The first timer runs the `refreshClock` callback after one second. The `refreshClock` callback triggers a re-render that creates a new timer running the `refreshClock` callback and so on.

Starting the Timer Once

We need to create the timer only once when the component is first rendered.

How can we do that?

Remember that when passing an empty array as the second argument to the effect hook it runs the given callback function only once.

```
useEffect(() => {
  const timerId = setInterval(refreshClock, 1000);
}, []);
```

Some effects require clean-ups, like our timer. When the component unmounts we need to stop the timer.

If the effect callback returns a function, that function is used to clean up resources when the component unmounts.

In our case, when the component unmounts the timer is stopped using the `clearInterval` utility.

```
useEffect(() => {
  const timerId = setInterval(refreshClock, 1000);
  return function cleanup() {
    clearInterval(timerId);
  };
}, []);
```

Below is the full `Clock` component.

```
import { useState, useEffect } from 'react';

function Clock(){
  const [date, setDate] = useState(new Date());
```

```
function refreshClock() {
  setDate(new Date());
}

useEffect(() => {
  const timerId = setInterval(refreshClock, 1000);
  return function cleanup() {
    clearInterval(timerId);
  };
}, []);

return (
  <span>
    {date.toLocaleTimeString()}
  </span>
);
}

export default Clock;
```

Key Notes

- The callbacks passed to the timer utility functions are closures around the value of the state. They point to the value of the state at the moment of their creation.
- The best practice is to update the state by providing an updater function to the state setter function. The updater function gives access to the current state value.

Chapter 13: Fetching Data

Retrieving data from a REST API is a common task we may encounter. We will look at a straightforward example and discuss what it means to do state management in such a case.

We are going to use a simple fake API for retrieving photos. The URL can be stored as a constant as it does not change.

```
const photosAPI =
  "https://jsonplaceholder.typicode.com/photos";
```

A retrieved photo object looks like the one below.

```
{
  "id": 1,
  "title": "accusamus beatae ad facilis",
  "url": "https://via.placeholder.com/600/92c952",
  "thumbnailUrl": "https://via.placeholder.com/150/92c952"
}
```

Rendering the List of Objects

Let's start building the list component that renders the array of photos.

The list component maps each object to a `<img>` element.

```
function Photos() {
  const photos = [];

  return (
    <div>
      {photos.map((photo) => (
        <img
          key={photo.id}
```

```
            src={photo.thumbnailUrl}
            alt={photo.title} />
        ))}
      </div>
  );
}
```

```
export default Photos;
```

Wait! Is the photos array correctly defined?

Let's think about it. We may start with an empty array, but after getting the list of photo objects from the REST API we need to change it. So what kind of variable is `photos`?

It is a state variable. It holds data that can be modified and the change is reflected on the screen.

```
import { useState } from "react";
```

```
// ...
const [photos, setPhotos] = useState([]);
```

Fetching Data

Next, let's fetch the photo objects. For this, we can simply use the `fetch` built-in utility. It returns a promise that gives access to the response data.

```
fetch(photosAPI)
  .then((response) => response.json());
```

Note that we need to extract the list of objects from the response. We do that using the `json` method available on the response object.

Once we have the new list of photo objects we update the state data using the setter function (`setPhotos`).

```
fetch(photosAPI)
  .then((response) => response.json())
  .then(setPhotos);
```

Is this enough? Should we leave the code like this?

Remember that the setter function updating the state data invokes again the list component. The component does again the fetch call. When the fetch finishes the setter function is called. The setter invokes again the list component. The component calls the fetch function and so on. This creates an endless loop.

The fetch call should be made only once when the list component is first rendered. How can we do that?

We use the effect hook with an empty array as its dependency.

```
import { useEffect, useState } from "react";
```

```
// ...
useEffect(() => {
  fetch(photosAPI)
    .then((response) => response.json())
    .then(setPhotos);
}, []);
```

Below is the full code of the list component.

```
import { useEffect, useState } from "react";

function Photos() {
  const [photos, setPhotos] = useState([]);

  useEffect(() => {
    fetch(photosAPI)
      .then((response) => response.json())
      .then(setPhotos);
  }, []);

  return (
    <div>
      {photos.map((photo) => (
        <img
          key={photo.id}
          src={photo.thumbnailUrl}
          alt={photo.title} />
      ))}
    </div>
  );
}
```

```
export default Photos;
```

Key Notes

- The data retrieved from the server should be saved as state. Such an array is initially empty and is updated once the data is got from the backend.
- When we need to make the fetch call only once, the effect hook is used with an empty array as its dependency.

Chapter 14: Searching

In this chapter, we analyze another common scenario, the search inside a list. This feature can be implemented both on the client side and on the server side. We look at the state management in both of these cases.

Not all APIs permit searching so we are going to use a fake one that enables such a functionality. We will search for products.

```
https://dummyjson.com/products
```

Search Component

We need a component that allows the user to type the search criteria. It contains a search input and a button.

```
function Search() {
  return (
    <form>
      <input type="search" />
      <button type="button">
        Search
      </button>
    </form>
  );
}
```

```
export default Search;
```

Is there any state needed for this component?

Yes, as always we have to define an associated state for the search input.

```
const [search, setSearch] = useState("");
```

```
// ...
<input
  type="search"
  value={search}
  onChange={(e) => setSearch(e.target.value)}
/>
```

What about events?

The component needs to communicate the final search text to the parent components. For this, it takes the onSearch callback as input.

```
function Search({ onSearch }) {}
```

When the form is submitted the onSearch callback is invoked and the current search text is passed as an argument.

```
const submitSearch = () => {
  onSearch(search);
};
```

```
// ...
<button type="button" onClick={submitSearch}>
  Search
</button>
```

Below is the full search component.

```
import { useState } from "react";

function Search({ onSearch }) {
  const [search, setSearch] = useState("");

  const submitSearch = () => {
    onSearch(search);
  };

  return (
    <form>
      <input
        type="search"
        value={search}
        onChange={(e) => setSearch(e.target.value)}
      />
```

```
        <button type="button" onClick={submitSearch}>
          Search
        </button>
      </form>
  );
}

export default Search;
```

Rendering the List

Now let's focus on rendering the list of products.

Below is an example of a product object.

```
{
  "id":1,
  "title":"iPhone 9",
  "description":"An apple mobile which is nothing like apple",
  "price":549,
  "brand":"Apple",
  "thumbnail":
    "https://i.dummyjson.com/products/1/thumbnail.jpg",
}
```

As pointed out several times, we can map such a list into a new list of UI elements.

```
{products
  .map((product) => (
    <div key={product.id}>
      <div>{product.title}</div>
      <img src={product.thumbnail} alt={product.title} />
    </div>
))}
```

Even better, we can extract the product details markup into its own component.

```
function Details({ product }) {
  return (
    <div key={product.id}>
      <div>{product.title}</div>
      <img src={product.thumbnail} alt={product.title} />
```

```
    </div>
  );
}
```

```
export default Details;
```

Then we can use such an item component to render the products inside the list component.

```
{ products.map((product) => (
  <Details key={product.id} product={product} />
))}
```

Fetching Data

The products component fetches the products and then renders them. Is there any state data needed?

No matter how the search is done, the list is initially empty. When the data is retrieved from the API the list is updated. The list of products should be stored as state data.

```
const [products, setProducts] = useState([]);
```

The fetch is done only once, when the page renders, using the effect hook with an empty dependency array.

```
useEffect(() => {
  fetch(`https://dummyjson.com/products`)
    .then((response) => response.json())
    .then((productsResponse) =>
      setProducts(productsResponse.products));
}, []);
```

Notice that depending on the API response we can get the result in different properties. In this case, the response looks something like the one below.

```
{
  products: [],
  total: 100
}
```

So in order to get the list of products we need to access the **products** property on the result object.

.then((productsResponse) => setProducts(productsResponse.products));

Below is the products component so far.

```
import { useEffect, useState } from "react";
import Search from "./Search";

function Products() {
  const [products, setProducts] = useState([]);

  useEffect(() => {
    fetch(`https://dummyjson.com/products`)
      .then((response) => response.json())
      .then((productsResponse) =>
        setProducts(productsResponse.products));
  }, []);

  return (
    <div>
      <Search />
      {products
        .map((product) => (
          <Details key={product.id} product={product} />
        ))}
    </div>
  );
}

export default Products;
```

Client-Side Search

Let's see what the search on the client side works like.

Searching on the client side implies getting all the products and filtering the result.

Consider a list of product objects. Here is how we can apply a search on it. We use the array `filter` method. The `toLowerCase` method is used to make the search insensitive.

```
products
  .filter((product) =>
```

```
    product.title.toLowerCase()
      .includes(search.toLowerCase())
  )
```

We can improve the previous code by extracting the filtering logic in its own function.

```
function byTitle(search) {
  return function (product) {
    return product.title.toLowerCase()
      .includes(search.toLowerCase());
  };
}
```

Now, in order to filter on the products list we use the `byTitle` function.

```
products.filter(byTitle(search))
```

The products component uses the search form to get the search text and then renders the list of products applying that filter criteria

Let's think about the state related to the search text inside the products component. Is there any state needed?

Inside the search component, there is an internal state storing the current search input value. This is not the same as the submitted search value. The user can type something, click the search button, and then type something else.

In the products component, we need a new state variable storing the submitted search value.

```
const [search, setSearch] = useState("");
```

```
//...
<Search onSearch={setSearch} />
```

Below is the complete code of the products component.

```
import { useEffect, useState } from "react";
import Search from "./Search";

function Products() {
  const [products, setProducts] = useState([]);
  const [search, setSearch] = useState("");
```

```
useEffect(() => {
  fetch(`https://dummyjson.com/products`)
    .then((response) => response.json())
    .then((productsResponse) =>
      setProducts(productsResponse.products));
}, []);

return (
  <div>
    <Search onSearch={setSearch} />
    {products
      .filter(byTitle(search))
      .map((product) => (
        <Details key={product.id} product={product} />
      ))}
  </div>
);
}
```

```
export default Products;
```

Server-Side Search

Searching on the server side involves the server performing the search and the client displaying that result. Also, the client needs to include the search criteria in the API request.

In our case, the API requires the search criteria in the query string of the request. Below is an example.

```
`https://dummyjson.com/products/search?q=${search}`
```

We already have the search criteria stored as state. We just have to use it when building the API request URL.

```
useEffect(() => {
  fetch(`https://dummyjson.com/products/search?q=${search}`)
    .then((response) => response.json())
    .then((productsResult) =>
      setProducts(productsResult.products));
}, []);
```

The issue with the previous code is that it does the API request only once when the component is first rendered. How can we make the request every time the search text changes?

We need the search variable in the dependency array (`[search]`) provided to the effect hook.

```
useEffect(() => {
    fetch(`https://dummyjson.com/products/search?q=${search}`)
      .then((response) => response.json())
      .then((productsResult) =>
        setProducts(productsResult.products));
  }, [search]);
```

Below is the full component code.

```
import { useEffect, useState } from "react";
import Search from "./Search";
import Details from "./Details";

function Products() {
  const [products, setProducts] = useState([]);
  const [search, setSearch] = useState("");

  useEffect(() => {
    console.log({ search });

    fetch(`https://dummyjson.com/products/search?q=${search}`)
      .then((response) => response.json())
      .then((productsResult) =>
        setProducts(productsResult.products));
  }, [search]);

  return (
    <div>
      <Search onSearch={setSearch} />
      {products.map((product) => (
        <Details key={product.id} product={product} />
      ))}
    </div>
  );
}
```

```
export default Products;
```

Key Notes

- Searching implies saving the current search criteria as state.
- Searching on the client side means retrieving all the data and then using the array `filter` method.
- Searching on the server side implies sending the search criteria to the server and letting it do the search.

Chapter 15: Pagination

Sometimes when fetching data, the backend API returns just one page of data at a time. Next, we are going to look at how to manage the state when dealing with a pagination system.

We will use a fake API. It allows us to retrieve the given page and also to specify the page size.

Here is an example of the API request for retrieving the first page. The page contains ten items.

```
https://api.instantwebtools.net/v1/passenger?page=0&size=10
```

Fetching the First Page

We start by fetching the first page and displaying those items on the screen.

The fake API URL can be stored in a constant.

```
const URL =
'https://api.instantwebtools.net/v1/passenger?page=0&size=10';
```

What about the list of retrieved items? How should it be stored?

The data retrieved from the API is stored in a state variable. This variable is initialized with an empty array.

```
const [list, setList] = useState([]);
```

The data is fetched only once when the component is rendered. This is accomplished using the effect hook.

Once the data is got from the backend the state is updated with the new list.

```
import React, { useEffect, useState } from "react";

function List() {
  const [list, setList] = useState([]);

  useEffect(() => {
    fetch(URL)
      .then((rsp) => rsp.json())
      .then((rsp) => setList(rsp.data));
  }, []);

  return (
    <div>
      {list.map((item) => (
        <div>{item.name}</div>
      ))}
    </div>
  );
}

export default List;
```

Setting the Current Page

The next step in implementing a pagination system requires storing and managing the current page. The current page starts from 0 in our case, and is incremented or decremented using the next and prev buttons.

```
const [page, setPage] = useState(0);

const nextPage = () => {
  setPage((page) => page + 1);
};

const prevPage = () => {
  setPage((page) => page - 1);
};

// ...
<div>Page: {page}</div>
<button onClick={prevPage}>Prev</button>
```

```
<button onClick={nextPage}>Next</button>
```

The **page** state variable stores the current page. The **prevPage** and **nextPage** handler functions update the state variable using the **setPage** setter function.

Fetching the Current Page Data

Let's now fetch the data for the current page.

First, we remove the page part from the base URL constant. This part is appended later when fetching the page data.

```
const URL =
  "https://api.instantwebtools.net/v1/passenger?size=10";
```

Instead of retrieving the data only when the component is first rendered, we are going to fetch the data each time the page changes. That implies modifying the dependency array of the **useEffect** hook to [page].

```
useEffect(() => {}, [page]);
```

Another change we need to make is the one for computing the current API URL. Basically, we append the current page to the existing URL constant.

```
`${URL}&page=${page}`
```

Here is the code structure so far.

```
import React, { useEffect, useState } from "react";

function List() {
  const [list, setList] = useState([]);
  const [page, setPage] = useState(0);

  useEffect(() => {
    fetch(`${URL}&page=${page}`)
      .then((rsp) => rsp.json())
      .then((rsp) => setList(rsp.data));
  }, [page]);

  const nextPage = () => {};
  const prevPage = () => {};
```

```
  return ();
}
```

```
export default List;
```

Disabling the Prev and Next Buttons

At the moment the next button can be clicked even after reaching the maximum number of pages. The prev button can be clicked even if we are on the first page. Let's fix that and disable these buttons when necessary.

The condition logic for disabling the prev button is simple. We just need to check if the current page is 0.

```
<button disabled={page === 0} onClick={prevPage}>
   Prev
</button>
```

In order to disable the next button, we need to know the total number of pages. This is a piece of information that should be got from the API.

We start by declaring the state variable for storing the total number of pages and initialize it with 1.

```
const [totalPages, setTotalPages] = useState(1);
```

Then, when the result is retrieved from the API, we set both the current page data and the total number of pages.

```
useEffect(() => {
    fetch(`${URL}&page=${page}`)
      .then((rsp) => rsp.json())
      .then((rsp) => {
        setTotalPages(rsp.totalPages);
        setList(rsp.data);
      });
  }, [page]);
```

Once we have the total number of pages the condition logic for disabling the next button is straightforward.

```
<button disabled={page > totalPages - 1} onClick={nextPage}>
   Next
</button>
```

Below is the complete code.

```jsx
import React, { useEffect, useState } from "react";

const URL =
  "https://api.instantwebtools.net/v1/passenger?size=10";

function List() {
  const [list, setList] = useState([]);
  const [page, setPage] = useState(0);
  const [totalPages, setTotalPages] = useState(1);

  useEffect(() => {
    fetch(`${URL}&page=${page}`)
      .then((rsp) => rsp.json())
      .then((rsp) => {
        setTotalPages(rsp.totalPages);
        setList(rsp.data);
      });
  }, [page]);

  const nextPage = () => {
    setPage((page) => page + 1);
  };

  const prevPage = () => {
    setPage((page) => page - 1);
  };

  return (
    <div>
      {list.map((item) => (
        <div key={item._id}>{item.name}</div>
      ))}
      <div>Page: {page}</div>
      <button
       disabled={page === 0}
       onClick={prevPage}>
         Prev
      </button>
      <button
       disabled={page >= totalPages - 1}
```

```
      onClick={nextPage}>
        Next
      </button>
    </div>
  );
}
```

```
export default List;
```

Loading More

Next, let's think about how to implement a load more system using the same API.

The prev and next buttons and their handlers should be removed. We just use a load more button.

```
const loadMore = () => {}
```

```
// ...
<button onClick={loadMore}>Load More</button>
```

What should the `loadMore` handler do?

It should load the next page of data. Basically, it increments the page number.

```
const loadMore = () => {
  setPage((page) => page + 1);
};
```

The difference comes when getting the result. The load more system displays more data to the user. It does not just show a new page. This time, instead of replacing the data in the state variable we add the new items to the existing list.

```
[...list, ...rsp.data]
```

Below is the effect hook doing the fetch and updating the list of items.

```
useEffect(() => {
  fetch(`${URL}&page=${page}`)
    .then((rsp) => rsp.json())
    .then((rsp) => {
      setTotalPages(rsp.totalPages);
```

```
      setList((list) => [...list, ...rsp.data]);
    });
}, [page]);
```

Another thing we should do is to disable load more when there are no more pages to load. This is straightforward. When the current page is larger than the available number of pages the load more button is disabled.

```
<button
onClick={loadMore}
disabled={page >= totalPages - 1}>
  Load More
</button>
```

Below is the full code.

```
import React, { useEffect, useState } from "react";

const URL =
  "https://api.instantwebtools.net/v1/passenger?size=10";

function List() {
  const [list, setList] = useState([]);
  const [page, setPage] = useState(0);
  const [totalPages, setTotalPages] = useState(3);

  useEffect(() => {
    fetch(`${URL}&page=${page}`)
      .then((rsp) => rsp.json())
      .then((rsp) => {
        setTotalPages(rsp.totalPages);
        setList((list) => [...list, ...rsp.data]);
      });
  }, [page]);

  const loadMore = () => {
    setPage((page) => page + 1);
  };

  return (
    <div>
      {list.map((item) => (
```

```
        <div key={item._id}>{item.name}</div>
      ))}
      <div>Page: {page}</div>
      <button
       onClick={loadMore}
       disabled={page >= totalPages - 1}>
         Load More
      </button>
    </div>
  );
}
```

```
export default List;
```

Key Notes

- When enabling a pagination system the current page needs to be stored as state data.
- A new API request is made each time the page changes and the current page is sent as part of the API request.
- The effect hook is used to detect when the page changes and do a new fetch call.
- The total number of pages should also be stored as state data for disabling the next button.
- Loading more data needs to store the current page and the total number of pages.
- When loading more data we add the newly retrieved data to the previously stored list instead of replacing it.

Chapter 16: Modal Component

In this chapter, we will look at what it means to create a modal dialog. The focus is still on the state management required to implement such a functionality.

Confirmation Modal

Let's start by implementing a simple confirmation modal. It shows a confirmation message to the user and has two buttons. One button confirms the choice and the other cancels it.

```
function ConfirmationModal() {
  return (
    <div>
      <div>
        <div>Are you sure?</div>
        <div>
          <button>Ok</button>
          <button>Cancel</button>
        </div>
      </div>
    </div>
  );
}
```

```
export default ConfirmationModal;
```

How should the modal component communicate with the parent components? How does the parent component know that either the confirm button or the cancel button has been clicked?

The modal dialog should take in two callbacks. One is to be called on the cancel click and the other is for the confirm click.

```
function ConfirmationModal({ onConfirm, onCancel }) {}
```

Here is the confirmation modal handling the click events using the provided callbacks.

```
function ConfirmationModal({ onConfirm, onCancel }) {
  return (
    <div>
      <div>
        <div>Are you sure?</div>
        <div>
          <button onClick={onConfirm}>Yes</button>
          <button onClick={onCancel}>No</button>
        </div>
      </div>
    </div>
  );
}


export default ConfirmationModal;
```

Styling

The confirmation modal should be shown over the normal document flow. In the standard document flow the block elements, like the ones created by the <div> tags, are displayed one below the other.

The modal displays an overlay over the existing layout using a fixed position element. Such an element is positioned relative to the window and remains in the same place when the page is scrolled. That overlay takes the entire page (left:0; top:0; width: 100%; height: 100%;) and has a transparent color (backgroundColor: "rgba(0,0,0,0.4)").

The box showing the confirmation question and the two buttons is centered using a flex container (display: "flex"). The center value aligns the flex item at the center of the container (align-items: "center"; justify-content: "center").

```
import React from "react";
```

```
const modalStyle = {
  position: "fixed",
  zIndex: 1,
  left: 0,
  top: 0,
  width: "100%",
  height: "100%",
  backgroundColor: "rgba(0,0,0,0.4)",
  display: "flex",
  alignItems: "center",
  justifyContent: "center"
};

function ConfirmationModal({ onConfirm, onCancel }) {
  return (
    <div style={modalStyle}>
      <div>
        <div>Are you sure?</div>
        <div>
          <button onClick={onConfirm}>Yes</button>
          <button onClick={onCancel}>No</button>
        </div>
      </div>
    </div>
  );
}

export default ConfirmationModal;
```

State Management

Now that we have a modal component, let's think about the state data required to handle it.

What is the use of the confirmation modal?

It appears when the user clicks a button and it closes when the confirm or the cancel buttons are clicked. Basically, the modal can either be opened or closed.

How the opened/closed status can be expressed using state data?

We can store the status (opened/closed) using a boolean.

```
const [show, setShow] = useState(false);
```

When the modal is opened the state variable is set to `true`. When the modal is closed the state variable is set to `false`.

```
const showModal = () => setShow(true);
const closeModal = () => setShow(false);
```

Conditional rendering is used to display the modal component only when the `show` state variable is `true`.

```
{show && <ConfirmationModal onCancel={closeModal} />}
```

Below is the full code of a sample component using the confirmation modal.

```
import { useState } from "react";
import ConfirmationModal from "./ConfirmationModal";

function Example() {
  const [show, setShow] = useState(false);

  const showModal = () => setShow(true);
  const closeModal = () => setShow(false);

  return (
    <div>
      <button onClick={showModal}>Show</button>
      {show && <ConfirmationModal onCancel={closeModal} />}
    </div>
  );
}


export default Example;
```

Key Notes

- The confirmation dialog is displayed over the existing document flow using CSS techniques like fixed positioning.
- The status, shown or hidden, of the confirmation dialog, is stored as a boolean state value.
- The dialog is shown and hidden using conditional rendering.

Chapter 17: Asking for Delete Confirmation

We built a confirmation modal. Next, we are going to integrate it into the Todo application. When the user presses the delete button, a confirmation dialog will be displayed asking for a confirmation action before deleting the selected item.

Integrating the Confirmation Modal

First, we need the confirmation modal inside the Todo application. It can be included the **App** root component.

```
import ConfirmationModal from "./ConfirmationModal";
```

Showing and hiding are done similarly to what we were doing before. A boolean state variable is required.

```
const [show, setShow] = useState(false);
```

```
const showModal = () => setShow(true);
const closeModal = () => setShow(false);
```

The confirmation modal is displayed when the **show** variable is **true** using condition rendering.

```
import { useState, useReducer } from "react";
import todosReducer, { initialTodos } from "./reducer";

import ConfirmationModal from "./ConfirmationModal";
import TodoForm from "./TodoForm";
import TodoList from "./TodoList";
```

```
function App() {
  const [list, dispatch] =
    useReducer(todosReducer, initialTodos);
  const [show, setShow] = useState(false);

  const showModal = () => setShow(true);
  const closeModal = () => setShow(false);

  return (
    <div>
      <TodoForm onAdd={() => {}} />
      <TodoList todos={list} onDelete={showModal} />
      {show && (
        <ConfirmationModal
          onCancel={closeModal}
          onConfirm={() => {
            console.log("delete id");
          }}
        />
      )}
    </div>
  );
}
```

```
export default App;
```

Deleting the Selected Item

Ok, we managed to show and hide the confirmation modal. What is missing is the actual deletion of the todo when the ok button is pressed.

The confirmation modal does not know what item to delete. It just triggers the onConfirm event when the ok button is pressed.

So how do we know what item to delete?

When opening the modal we also need to store the selected item.

```
const [selectedId, setSelectedId] = useState(0);
```

Below is a new handler function that first sets the selected todo and then opens the confirmation modal. This is the handler for the onDelete event on the TodoList component.

```
const showModalAndSelectId = (id) => {
  setSelectedId(id);
  showModal();
};
```

```
//...
<TodoList todos={list} onDelete={showModalAndSelectId} />
```

We need another handler function that deletes the selected todo and then closes the confirmation modal. This is the handler for the `onConfirm` event on the modal.

```
const closeModalAndDeleteSelectedId = () => {
  deleteTodo(selectedId);
  closeModal();
};
```

```
//...
<ConfirmationModal
  onCancel={closeModal}
  onConfirm={closeModalAndDeleteSelectedId}
/>
```

Here is the full code of the `App` component using the confirmation modal.

```
import { useReducer, useState } from "react";
import todosReducer, { initialTodos } from "./reducer";

import ConfirmationModal from "./ConfirmationModal";
import TodoForm from "./TodoForm";
import TodoList from "./TodoList";

function App() {
  const [list, dispatch] =
    useReducer(todosReducer, initialTodos);
  const [show, setShow] = useState(false);
  const [selectedId, setSelectedId] = useState(0);

  const addTodo = (name) => {
    dispatch({ type: "addTodo", payload: name });
  };
```

```
const deleteTodo = (id) => {
  dispatch({ type: "deleteTodo", payload: id });
};

const showModal = () => setShow(true);
const closeModal = () => setShow(false);

const showModalAndSelectId = (id) => {
  setSelectedId(id);
  showModal();
};

const closeModalAndDeleteSelectedId = () => {
  deleteTodo(selectedId);
  closeModal();
};

return (
  <div>
    <TodoForm onAdd={addTodo} />
    <TodoList todos={list} onDelete={showModalAndSelectId} />
    {show && (
      <ConfirmationModal
        onCancel={closeModal}
        onConfirm={closeModalAndDeleteSelectedId}
      />
    )}
  </div>
);
}

export default App;
```

Context API

Things are looking good, but what about extracting this logic related to the confirmation modal outside of the component?

Next, we discuss how to put this logic in what is called the context.

Wait, one question! Why do we need this Context API system at all? Don't we already have the custom hook option for encapsulating custom logic?

When using a custom hook encapsulating the state hook, it creates a new internal state each time is used. For example, using the custom hook inside the `App` root component creates an internal state in that component. Using the same custom hook inside the `TodoItem` component creates a new internal state. We don't want this behavior in our case. We want to use the same confirmation modal state logic in all the todo components.

The Context API allows the creation of a single instance of the state data somewhere in the tree of components. This place where the state data is created is defined by the usage of what is called the context provider component. All the child components starting from that level in the tree have access to the same state data.

Let's put the modal related logic in context. This will help with understanding this API.

Extracting the Logic in the Context

Here is the logic associated with the usage of the confirmation modal.

```
const [show, setShow] = useState(false);
const [selectedId, setSelectedId] = useState(0);

const showModal = () => setShow(true);
const closeModal = () => setShow(false);

const showModalAndSelectId = (id) => {
  setSelectedId(id);
  showModal();
};
```

Context

First, we need to create the context object. This is done using the `createContext` utility function.

```
import { createContext } from "react";

const ModalContext = createContext({});
```

In order to access the context inside a component we need the `useContext`hook. A better option though is to create a wrapper custom hook around it and add some additional logic.

```
import { createContext, useContext } from "react";

const ModalContext = createContext({});

const useModalContext = () => {
  const context = useContext(ModalContext);
  if (!context) {
    throw new Error("Missing ContextProvider");
  }
  return context;
};
```

```
export { ModalContext, useModalContext };
```

The `useContext` hook takes a context object and returns the current context value. The context object is the one built using the `createContext` utility.

The current context value is the one provided in the `value` property of the nearest `<Context.Provider>` component in the tree.

Provider

Context objects come with a `Provider` component that allows other components to use the context.

Below is our custom provider encapsulating the context related logic. It returns the `ModalContext.Provider` component. The `Provider` component takes a `value` prop. All the logic we want to expose goes into this `value` property.

All the consuming components, descendants of this `Provider` component can access this `value` property.

```
import { useState } from "react";
import { ModalContext } from "./ModalContext";

const ModalContextProvider = ({ children }) => {
  const [show, setShow] = useState(false);
  const [selectedId, setSelectedId] = useState(0);

  const showModal = () => setShow(true);
```

```
  const closeModal = () => setShow(false);

  const showModalAndSelectId = (id) => {
    setSelectedId(id);
    showModal();
  };

  const value = {
    show,
    selectedId,
    showModalAndSelectId,
    closeModal
  };

  return (
    <ModalContext.Provider value={value}>
      {children}
    </ModalContext.Provider>
  );
};

export default ModalContextProvider;
```

Using the Modal Context

Now we can use the useModalContext hook inside the App component and have access to all the exposed data and functions.

```
import { useModalContext } from "./ModalContext";

function App() {
  //...

  const {
    show,
    selectedId,
    showModalAndSelectId,
    closeModal
  } = useModalContext();

  return ();
```

```
}
```

```
export default App;
```

The context logic can be accessed in all the child components of the provider component. We can use it in the item component for example.

```
import { useModalContext } from "./ModalContext";
```

```jsx
function TodoItem({ todo }) {
  const { showModalAndSelectId } = useModalContext();

  return (
    <li>
      {todo.name} 
      <button
       onClick={() => showModalAndSelectId(todo.id)}>
         Delete
      </button>
    </li>
  );
}
```

```
export default TodoItem;
```

Key Notes

- When using a modal component we may need to store additional state data for managing its events. For example, we may need to keep the selected item in the list.
- The modal related logic, like for showing, hiding, and selecting an item can be encapsulated inside a custom context.
- The state data encapsulated in a context is unique for each instance of `Context.Provider` component. When there is only one instance of the `Provider` component we can consider that state global.

Chapter 18: Takeaways

In the last chapter, we will review the primary practices for managing state in React.

Many examples used the state hook for defining the internal state. This can be considered the main hook for representing the state. The other hook used was the reducer hook. It required a reducer function to manage its state. It guided us to identify the managing state logic and extracted it into a reducer function.

Next, a few essential things about state management are pointed out.

Don't create a state variable when it can be computed

Consider the following example where we need to disable a button when the state variable is empty. In this case, we can just decide on the fly the value of the `disabled` property.

```
const [state, setState] = useState('');

<button disabled={state === ''}>Click</button>
```

We can also save the result in a simple variable and use it for the `disabled` property.

```
const [state, setState] = useState('');

const disabled = state === '';
<button disabled={disabled}>Click</button>
```

Don't create a new state variable when it can be computed from other state variables. Taking such an approach will lead to unnecessary synchronization logic and unnecessary re-rendering. In our example, we need to change the value of the `disabled` state variable when the other `state` variable changes. Don't do the following, keep it simple.

```
const [state, setState] = useState('');
const [disabled, setDisable] = useState('');

useEffect(()=> {
  setDisable(state === '');
}, [state])

<button disabled={disabled}>Click</button>
```

Use the setter function, not the read variable

The state hook returns a variable and a setter function. Don't use the variable to update the state.

```
const [state, setState] = useState(0);

//This is wrong
state = 1;
```

That change is not detected, and the component does not re-render to show the difference. Always use the setter function (`setState`) to update the state.

The same applies to the reducer hook. Don't use the variable to update the state data, use the `dispatch` function.

Treat the state value as being immutable

Also, pay attention to not mutating objects.

The state of course changes. That is the point of the state data, to be changed. Nonetheless, the value of the state should be treated as being immutable.

That is not a problem with primitives values, they are immutable anyway. The problem appears when dealing with objects. Objects in JavaScript are not immutable.

When mutating the state value, React's diffing algorithm does not detect the change and the component does not update correctly.

```
const [state, setState] = useState({value: 0});
```

```
//This is wrong
state.value = 1;
setState(state)
```

Using immutable values means creating a changed copy.

```
setState({ ...state, value: 1})
```

Use an updater function

When computing the new state based on the current state use an updater function.

Remember the example for the timer example.

```
const [count, setCount] = useState(0);

useEffect(() => {
  setTimeout(() => {
    setCount(count + 100);
  }, 5000);
}, []);
```

The count variable inside the timeout callback does not point to the latest value. The timer callback creates a closure around the initial value of the count variable.

The updater function always points to the current state value. The best way to update the state is to provide an updater function. The updater function takes the previous state as the argument and computes the new state.

In our example count => count + 100 is the updater function.

```
useEffect(() => {
  setTimeout(() => {
    setCount((count) => count + 100);
  }, 5000);
}, []);
```

Don't access the state after using the setter function

The setter function (setState) is an asynchronous function. This means it is not guaranteed to have the result of its usage on the next line.

```
const [state, setState] = useState(0);

const handleChange = () => {
  setState(1)
  console.log(state);
}
```

Use the effect hook to detect changes in the state variable.

```
const [state, setState] = useState(0);

useEffect(()=>{
  console.log(state);
}, [state]);
```

Use controlled inputs

The best practice is to work with controlled inputs in a form. That means associating inputs with state variables.

Here is the name state variable associated with the name input.

```
const [name, setName] = useState('');

<input
type="text"
value={name}
onChange={(e) => setName(e.target.value)}
/>
```

Consider extracting state related logic to be reused

Sometimes the state related logic can be reused. For example, the logic for managing form inputs or for doing validation can be reused for different forms.

Such functionality can be extracted in a custom hook. Remember the useForm hook structure.

```
import { useState } from "react";

function useForm(fields) {
  const [state, setState] = useState(fields);
```

```
  const setField = (e) => {};

  return [state, setField];
}

export default useForm;
```

Consider extracting state related logic to the context

The custom hooks encapsulating state hooks create a new instance of the state data on each usage. When the same state data should be accessed and modified in several components consider putting the reusable logic in context. Such an example is a confirmation modal that can be accessed by several components.

Key Notes

- The main hooks for defining state data are the state and reducer hooks.
- Don't create a new state variable when it can be computed from other stave variables. This leads to unnecessary synchronization logic and re-rendering.
- When updating the state data use the setter function, do not use the read variable.
- The value stored in the state variable should be considered immutable. This means creating a changed copy when modifying it.
- The best practice is to provide an updater function when modifying the state based on the previous value. The updater function takes the current state and returns the new state.
- Don't access the state data after using the setter function. The setter function is asynchronous and there is no guarantee to have the new state value on the next line. Use the effect hook to detect when a state variable changes.
- It is good practice to work with inputs as controlled inputs. That means associating the inputs' values with state data.
- Consider extracting state related logic that can be reused into custom hooks.
- Consider extracting state related logic to the context when the same data needs to be accessed and changed in several components.

Source Code

The project files from this book are available at
https://github.com/cristi-salcescu/state-management-with-react-hooks.

Feedback

I will be glad to hear your feedback. For comments, questions, or suggestions regarding this book send me an email to cristisalcescu@gmail.com.
Thanks in advance for considering to write a review of the book.

About the author

Cristian Salcescu is the author of Functional React.
He is a technical lead passionate about front-end development and enthusiastic about sharing ideas. He took different roles and participated in all parts of software creation.

Other books

Discover Functional JavaScript

An overview of Functional and Object Oriented Programming in JavaScript

Cristian Salcescu

For a more in-depth look at JavaScript and main functional principles, you may read 'Discover Functional JavaScript'. Here, you will find more on pure functions, immutability, currying, decorators but also ideas on how to make code easier to read. JavaScript brings functional programming to the mainstream and offers a new way of doing object-oriented programming without classes and prototypes.

Functional Programming in JavaScript

Cristian Salcescu

In the 'Functional Programming in JavaScript' book you will find how to use JavaScript as a functional programming language by disabling the 'this' keyword and enforcing immutable objects with a linter. You will learn how to use statements like 'if' and 'switch' in a functional way, or how to create and use functors and monads. It turns out that JavaScript has everything it needs to be used as a functional language. We just have to remove features from the language.

Functional React

THIRD EDITION

Quick start with React Hooks and Redux

Cristian Salcescu

If you want to learn how to build modern React applications using functional components and functional programming principles, you can consider reading 'Functional React, 2nd Edition'.

Functional Architecture
with React and Redux

Cristian Salcescu

Continue your learning path with 'Functional Architecture with React and Redux' book, and put in practice what you learned by building several applications with an incremental level of complexity.

The functional architecture implies getting the initial state, showing it to the user using the view functions, listening for actions, updating the state based on those actions, and rendering the updated state back to the user again.

Microblog React Project

Cristian Salcescu

The 'Microblog React Project' book takes a project-based learning approach by engaging you in building a practical application. The reader will learn things on the way by developing different parts of this project. The Microblog application will be built using React with Hooks and libraries like Redux, Redux Thunk, Redux Toolkit, Material UI, or Axios.

UI State Management
From Object-Oriented to Functional

Cristian Salcescu

The 'UI State Management' book gives you an overview of how state is managed by building a note-taking application with four different libraries. We start from an object-oriented approach using Svelte, centralize state with Vuex, then move to a functional approach with React and Redux, and in the end arrive at a solution using only pure functions with Elm.

Enjoy the learning journey!